A handbook of essential mathematical formulae

Alan Davies & Diane Crann

University of Hertfordshire Press

First published in Great Britain in 2004 by
University of Hertfordshire Press
Learning and Information Services
University of Hertfordshire
College Lane
Hatfield
Hertfordshire AL10 9AB

Reprinted in 2017, 2018

British Library Cataloguing in Publication Data
A catalogue record for this book is available from the British Library

ISBN 978-1-902806-41-9

Design by Diane Crann

Cover design by John Robertshaw, AL5 2JB

Printed in Great Britain by Hobbs the Printers Ltd, SO40 3WX

Contents

iv

Thoughout the handbook the symbol j is used for the unit imaginary number *i.e.* $j^2 = -1$ or $j = \sqrt{-1}$. Alternatively the symbol i is frequently used instead of j.

Chapter 1

Algebra, Trigonometry and Geometry

A *polynomial* of degree n is an expression of the form

$$P(x) = a_n x^n + a_{n-1} x^{n-1} + \ldots + a_2 x^2 + a_1 x^1 + a_0$$

Sigma $\displaystyle\sum_{i=1}^{n} a_i = a_1 + a_2 + a_3 + \ldots + a_{n-1} + a_n$

Factorial $n! = n(n-1)(n-2)\ldots 3.2.1$

Finite series

$$\sum_{k=1}^{n} k = \frac{1}{2}n(n+1)$$

$$\sum_{k=1}^{n} k^2 = \frac{1}{6}n(n+1)(2n+1)$$

$$\sum_{k=1}^{n} k^3 = \left(\sum_{k=1}^{n} k\right)^2 = \frac{1}{4}n^2(n+1)^2$$

1.1   Indices and logarithms

If $x > 0$ then we have the following properties:

$$x^0 = 1, \quad x^{-1} = 1/x, \quad x^{m+n} = x^m x^n, \quad x^{m-n} = x^m/x^n, \quad x^{mn} = (x^m)^n \quad x^{\frac{1}{n}} = \sqrt[n]{x}$$

If $a > 0$ and $a \neq 1$ then

$$\log_a 1 = 0, \quad \log_a(x^{-1}) = \log_a(1/x) = -\log_a x$$

$$\log_a x + \log_a y = \log_a(xy), \quad m\log_a x = \log_a(x^m)$$

$$\log_a x - \log_a y = \log_a(x/y)$$

The logarithm and power functions are *inverse functions, i.e.*

if $x = \log_a y$ then $y = a^x$

and if $x = a^y$ then $y = \log_a x$

Change of base $\log_a x = \log_b x / \log_b a$

Logarithms to base e, *i.e.* $\log_e x$, are often written $\ln x$. Such logarithms are called *natural logarithms*. e is the exponential constant given by

$e = 1 + \frac{1}{1!} + \frac{1}{2!} + \frac{1}{3!} + \ldots = 2.71828\ldots$

1.2 Factors and roots of equations

$(a \pm b)^2 = a^2 \pm 2ab + b^2$

$a^2 - b^2 = (a + b)(a - b)$

$a^3 \pm b^3 = (a \pm b)(a^2 \mp ab + b^2)$

$a^n - b^n = (a - b)(a^{n-1} + a^{n-2}b + a^{n-3}b^2 + \ldots + ab^{n-2} + b^{n-1})$

Quadratic equation $ax^2 + bx + c = 0$ with roots α, β

$$\alpha, \beta = \left[-b \pm \sqrt{b^2 - 4ac}\right]/2a$$

$$\alpha + \beta = -b/a, \quad \alpha\beta = c/a$$

Cubic equation $ax^3 + bx^2 + cx + d = 0$ with roots α, β, γ

$$\alpha + \beta + \gamma = -b/a, \quad \alpha\beta + \beta\gamma + \gamma\alpha = c/a, \quad \alpha\beta\gamma = -d/a$$

$f(a) = 0$ if and only if $(x - a)$ is a factor of $f(x)$.

Remainder Theorem

Suppose $P(x) = a_n x^n + a_{n-1} x^{n-1} + \ldots + a_1 x + a_0$ is a polynomial of degree n and that a is a root of the equation $P(x) = 0$. Then $(x - a)$ is a factor of $P(x)$.

1.3 Partial fractions

If the degree of the polynomial $f(x)$ is less than that of the denominator then:

$$\frac{f(x)}{(x + a)(x + b)\ldots} = \frac{A}{x + a} + \frac{B}{x + b} + \ldots$$

$$\frac{f(x)}{(ax^2 + bx + c)(dx + e)} = \frac{Ax + B}{ax^2 + bx + c} + \frac{C}{dx + e}$$

$$\frac{f(x)}{(ax + b)(cx + d)^2} = \frac{A}{ax + b} + \frac{B}{cx + d} + \frac{C}{(cx + d)^2}$$

1.4 Permutations and combinations

The number of ways of selecting r objects from n objects with due regard to order is

$$^nP_r = \frac{n!}{(n-r)!}$$

The number of ways of selecting r objects from n objects without regard to order is

$$\binom{n}{r} = \frac{n!}{(n-r)!\,r!} \quad \text{(sometimes written } ^nC_r)$$

Properties

$$\binom{n}{r} = \binom{n}{n-r}, \quad \binom{n+1}{r} = \binom{n}{r} + \binom{n}{r-1}$$

Binomial Theorem
For any positive integer, n,

$$(a+b)^n = \sum_{r=0}^{n} \binom{n}{r} a^{n-r}b^r$$

1.5 Trigonometric functions

Degrees and Radians
$360° = 2\pi \text{ rad} \quad 1° = \frac{\pi}{180} \text{ rad} \quad 1\,\text{rad} = \left(\frac{180}{\pi}\right)° \approx 57.296°$
$\cos n\pi = (-1)^n, \quad \sin n\pi = 0$

$\cos\left[(2n+1)\pi/2\right] = 0, \quad \sin\left[(2n+1)\pi/2\right] = (-1)^n$

$\cos(\pi/4) = \sin(\pi/4) = 1/\sqrt{2}$
$\cos(\pi/3) = \sin(\pi/6) = 1/2$
$\cos(\pi/6) = \sin(\pi/3) = \sqrt{3}/2$

$\cos(\pi/2 - \theta) = \sin\theta, \quad \sin(\pi/2 - \theta) = \cos\theta$

Trigonometric identities
$\cos^{-1}x = \pi/2 - \sin^{-1}x, \quad \tan^{-1}x = \pi/2 - \tan^{-1}(1/x)$

$\sin^2 x + \cos^2 x = 1,$
$1 + \tan^2 x = \sec^2 x$
$1 + \cot^2 x = \text{cosec}^2 x$

$\sin(x+y) = \sin x \cos y + \cos x \sin y$
$\sin(x-y) = \sin x \cos y - \cos x \sin y$

$$\cos{(x+y)} = \cos{x}\cos{y} - \sin{x}\sin{y}$$
$$\cos{(x-y)} = \cos{x}\cos{y} + \sin{x}\sin{y}$$

$$\tan{(x+y)} = \frac{\tan{x}+\tan{y}}{1-\tan{x}\tan{y}}$$
$$\tan{(x-y)} = \frac{\tan{x}-\tan{y}}{1+\tan{x}\tan{y}}$$

$$\cos 2x = \cos^2 x - \sin^2 x = 2\cos^2 x - 1 = 1 - 2\sin^2 x$$
$$\sin 2x = 2\sin x \cos x, \quad \tan 2x = \frac{2\tan x}{1-\tan^2 x}$$

$$\cos 3x = 4\cos^3 x - 3\cos x, \quad \sin 3x = 3\sin x - 4\sin^3 x$$

$$\sin x + \sin y = 2\sin\frac{x+y}{2}\cos\frac{x-y}{2}$$
$$\sin x - \sin y = 2\cos\frac{x+y}{2}\sin\frac{x-y}{2},$$

$$\cos x + \cos y = 2\cos\frac{x+y}{2}\cos\frac{x-y}{2}$$
$$\cos x - \cos y = -2\sin\frac{x+y}{2}\sin\frac{x-y}{2}$$

$$\cos x \cos y = \tfrac{1}{2}\left[\cos{(x+y)} + \cos{(x-y)}\right]$$
$$\sin x \sin y = \tfrac{1}{2}\left[\cos{(x-y)} - \cos{(x+y)}\right]$$
$$\sin x \cos y = \tfrac{1}{2}\left[\sin{(x+y)} + \sin{(x-y)}\right]$$

$$\cos^2 x = \tfrac{1}{2}\left(1+\cos 2x\right), \quad \sin^2 x = \tfrac{1}{2}\left(1-\cos 2x\right)$$

$$\sin^{-1} x \pm \sin^{-1} y = \sin^{-1}\left(x\sqrt{1-y^2} \pm y\sqrt{1-x^2}\right)$$
$$\cos^{-1} x \pm \cos^{-1} y = \cos^{-1}\left(xy \mp \sqrt{1-x^2}\sqrt{1-y^2}\right)$$
$$\tan^{-1} x \pm \tan^{-1} y = \tan^{-1}\left[(x \pm y)/(1 \mp xy)\right]$$

If $t = \tan\dfrac{x}{2}$, then

$$\sin x = \frac{2t}{1+t^2}, \quad \cos x = \frac{1-t^2}{1+t^2}, \quad \tan x = \frac{2t}{1-t^2}$$

$$\cos x = \left(e^{jx} + e^{-jx}\right)/2, \quad \sin x = \left(e^{jx} - e^{-jx}\right)/2j$$

De Moivre's Theorem

$$(\cos x + j\sin x)^n = \cos nx + j\sin nx$$

$$e^{jx} = \cos x + j\sin x, \quad e^{-jx} = \cos x - j\sin x$$

1.6 Hyperbolic functions

$$\cosh x = \left(e^x + e^{-x} \right)/2, \quad \sinh x = \left(e^x - e^{-x} \right)/2$$
$$e^x = \cosh x + \sinh x, \quad e^{-x} = \cosh x - \sinh x$$

$$\tanh x = \frac{\sinh x}{\cosh x} = \frac{e^x - e^{-x}}{e^x + e^{-x}} = \frac{e^{2x} - 1}{e^{2x} + 1} = \frac{1 - e^{-2x}}{1 + e^{-2x}}$$

$$\sinh^{-1} x = \ln\left(x + \sqrt{x^2 + 1} \right)$$

$$\cosh^{-1} x = \pm \ln\left(x + \sqrt{x^2 - 1} \right)$$

$$\tanh^{-1} x = \frac{1}{2} \ln\left(\frac{1 + x}{1 - x} \right)$$

Relationship with trigonometric functions

$$\cos jx = \cosh x, \quad \cosh jx = \cos x$$
$$\sin jx = j \sinh x, \quad \sinh jx = j \sin x$$

Osborne's rule

An identity involving hyperbolic functions may be obtained from the equivalent trigonometric identity by replacing the trigonometric functions with the corresponding hyperbolic functions and changing the sign of a product (or implied product) of *two* sines.

e.g.

$$\cosh^2 x - \sinh^2 x = 1, \quad 1 - \tanh^2 x = \text{sech}^2 x$$

N.B. The Maclaurin series in powers of x for the hyperbolic functions may be found from the Maclaurin series for the corresponding trigonometric function by changing the sign of a product of two x's

e.g.

$$\cosh x = 1 + \frac{x^2}{2!} + \frac{x^4}{4!} + \cdots + \frac{x^{2n}}{(2n)!} + \cdots$$

$$\sinh^{-1} x = x - \frac{x^3}{6} + \frac{3x^5}{40} - \frac{5x^7}{112} + \ldots + (-1)^n \frac{(2n)!}{2^{2n}(n!)^2} \frac{x^{2n+1}}{(2n+1)} + \cdots$$

1.7 Geometry

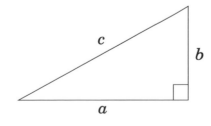

Pythagoras' theorem

$$a^2 + b^2 = c^2$$

Theorems

The angle sum of a triangle is $180°$ or π rad.

The sum of the interior angles of an n-sided polygon is $(2n - 4) \times 90°$ or $(n - 2)\pi$ rad.

The exterior angle of a triangle is equal to the sum of the interior opposite angles.

The angle subtended by a diameter at the circumference of a circle is $90°$.

The angle subtended by a chord at the centre of a circle is twice the angle subtended by the same chord in the opposite segment.

The diagonals of a parallelogram bisect each other.

1.8 Conic sections

A conic section is the locus of a point that moves in a plane so that the ratio (the eccentricity) of its distance from a fixed point (the focus) in the plane, to its distance from a fixed line (the directrix), is a constant, ϵ.

1. Parabola $(\epsilon = 1)$; focus at $(a, 0)$, directrix $x = -a$
   Cartesian equation: $y^2 = 4ax$
   Parametric equation: $x = at^2, y = 2at$

2. Ellipse $(\epsilon < 1)$; foci at $(\pm a\epsilon, 0)$, directrices $x = \pm a/\epsilon$
   Major axis of length $2a$, minor axis of length $2b$
   Cartesian equation: $\dfrac{x^2}{a^2} + \dfrac{y^2}{b^2} = 1$ with $b = a\left(1 - \epsilon^2\right)^{\frac{1}{2}}$
   Parametric equation: $x = a\cos\theta, y = b\sin\theta$

3. Hyperbola $(\epsilon > 1)$; foci at $(\pm a\epsilon, 0)$, directrices at $x = \pm a/\epsilon$
   Cartesian equation: $\dfrac{x^2}{a^2} - \dfrac{y^2}{b^2} = 1$ with $b = a\left(\epsilon^2 - 1\right)^{\frac{1}{2}}$
   Parametric equation: $x = a\sec\theta, y = b\tan\theta$
   Rectangular hyperbola referred to its asymptotes as axes: $xy = c^2$

4. Circle $(\epsilon = 0)$
   Cartesian equation $x^2 + y^2 = a^2$
   Parametric equation $x = a\cos\theta, y = a\sin\theta$

The polar equation for these three conic sections with the pole at a focus is

$$\frac{1}{r} = 1 + \epsilon \cos \theta$$

The general conic

The equation $ax^2 + 2hxy + by^2 + 2gx + 2fy + c = 0$ represents:

a circle if $a = b$ and $h = 0$

a pair of straight lines if $af^2 + bg^2 + ch^2 = 2fgh + abc$

a parabola if $h^2 = ab$

an ellipse if $h^2 < ab$

a hyperbola if $h^2 > ab$

a rectangular hyperbola if $a + b = 0$

1.9 Mensuration

Circle, radius r: perimeter is $2\pi r$, area is πr^2

For a segment of angular width θ (radians), arc length is $r\theta$ and area is $\frac{1}{2}r^2\theta$

Ellipse, axes $2a$ and $2b$: perimeter is approximately $2\pi\sqrt{(a^2 + b^2)/2}$,
    area is πab

Cylinder, radius r, height h: surface area is $2\pi r(h + r)$, volume is $\pi r^2 h$

Cone, base radius r, height h, slant height l:
    curved surface area is $\pi r l$, volume is $\pi r^2 h/3$

Sphere, radius r: area is $4\pi r^2$, volume is $4\pi r^3/3$,
    area cut off by parallel planes distance h apart is $2\pi r h$

Triangle, ABC sides a, b, c:
    area of triangle is
    $\Delta = \frac{1}{2}bc \sin A = \sqrt{s(s - a)(s - b)(s - c)}$, (*Heron's formula*)
    where $2s = a + b + c$

Radius of circumcircle is $R = abc/4\Delta$

Radius of inscribed circle is $r = \Delta/s$

sine rule $\dfrac{a}{\sin A} = \dfrac{b}{\sin B} = \dfrac{c}{\sin C} = 2R$

cosine rule $a^2 = b^2 + c^2 - 2bc \cos A$

$\sin(A/2) = \sqrt{\{(s - b)(s - c)/bc\}}$
$\cos(A/2) = \sqrt{\{(s - a)/bc\}}$

1.10 Complex numbers

The algebra of complex numbers follows the same rules as that for real numbers with the addition of the unit imaginary number j which has the property $j^2 = -1$ or $j = \sqrt{-1}$.

Cartesian form $z = x + jy$ where x is called the *real part* of z, Re(z), and y is called the *imaginary part* of z, Im(z).

The *Argand diagram* is a geometric representation of the complex number $z = x + jy$, the point (x, y) represents z.

Polar form $z = r(\cos\theta + j\sin\theta)$ where (r, θ) are the polar coordinates of (x, y)

Exponential form $z = re^{j\theta}$

Complex conjugate $\bar{z} = x - jy = r(\cos\theta - j\sin\theta) = re^{-j\theta}$

Modulus $|z| = \sqrt{x^2 + y^2}, \quad z\bar{z} = r^2 = x^2 + y^2$

Argument (principal value) $\arg z = \theta, \; (-\pi < \theta \leq \pi)$.

De Moivre's theorem $(\cos\theta + j\sin\theta)^n = \cos n\theta + j\sin n\theta$

Euler's formulae

$$e^{j\theta} = \cos\theta + j\sin\theta, \qquad e^{-j\theta} = \cos\theta - j\sin\theta$$
$$\cos\theta = \tfrac{1}{2}\left(e^{j\theta} + e^{-j\theta}\right), \quad \sin\theta = \tfrac{1}{2j}\left(e^{j\theta} - e^{-j\theta}\right)$$

Complex roots If $z = re^{j\theta}$ then the n complex roots of z are given by

$$z^{1/n} = r^{1/n}\exp\{j\frac{\theta + 2k\pi}{n}\} \quad k = 0, 1, 2, \ldots, n-1$$

These roots are equally spaced around the circle, radius $r^{1/n}$, centred on the origin.

Fundamental theorem of algebra

A polynomial, $P(z)$, of degree n given by

$$P(z) = a_n z^n + a_{n-1} z^{n-1} + \cdots + a_1 z + a_0 \quad (a_n \neq 0)$$

can be factorized into n complex factors:

$$P(z) = a_n (z - z_1)(z - z_2) \ldots (z - z_n).$$

The numbers $z_1, z_2, \ldots, z_n$ are called the *roots* of the equation $P(z) = 0$. If the coefficients $a_0, a_1, \ldots, a_n$ are all real then the complex roots occur in conjugate pairs.

8

Complex variable

If $f(z) = u(x,y) + jv(x,y)$ is an *analytic function* of the complex variable $z = x + jy$, then u and v satisfy the *Cauchy-Riemann equations*

$$\frac{\partial u}{\partial x} = \frac{\partial v}{\partial y} \qquad \frac{\partial u}{\partial y} = -\frac{\partial v}{\partial x}$$

1.11 Inequalities

Basic rules based on 'greater than' (the same rules apply to $>, <, \geq, \leq$)

$$x > y \Leftrightarrow x + a > y + a$$

$$\text{if } p > 0 \text{ then } x > y \Leftrightarrow px > py$$

$$\text{if } n < 0 \text{ then } x > y \Leftrightarrow nx < ny$$

$$\text{if } a > b \text{ and } x > y \text{ then } a + x > b + y$$

$$\text{if } x > y \text{ and } y > z \text{ then } x > z$$

$$\sqrt{x + y} \leq \sqrt{x} + \sqrt{y}$$

$$\text{if } x, y > 0 \text{ then } x < y \Leftrightarrow x^2 < y^2 \Leftrightarrow \sqrt{x} < \sqrt{y}$$

$$\text{if } x > 1 \text{ then } x^m > x^n \Leftrightarrow m > n$$

$$\text{if } 0 < x < 1 \text{ then } x^m > x^n \Leftrightarrow m < n$$

$$\text{if } x > 1 \text{ then } x^{1/m} > x^{1/n} \Leftrightarrow m > n$$

Bernoulli's inequality

$$\text{If } x > -1 \text{ then } (1 + x)^n \geq 1 + nx$$

Arithmetic mean $\frac{1}{2}(x + y)$ *Geometric mean* $\sqrt{xy}$

$$\tfrac{1}{2}(x + y) \geq \sqrt{xy}$$

Triangle inequality $|x + y| \leq |x| + |y|$

$$|x| - |y| \leq ||x| - |y|| \leq |x - y|$$

Cauchy Schwarz inequality $|\mathbf{u}.\mathbf{v}| \leq \|\mathbf{u}\|\|\mathbf{v}\|$
Minkowski inequality $\|\mathbf{u} + \mathbf{v}\| \leq \|\mathbf{u}\| + \|\mathbf{v}\|$

Chapter 2

Determinants and Matrices

2.1 Determinants

$$2 \times 2 : \begin{vmatrix} a & b \\ c & d \end{vmatrix} = ad - bc$$

$$3 \times 3 : \begin{vmatrix} a_{11} & a_{12} & a_{13} \\ a_{21} & a_{22} & a_{23} \\ a_{31} & a_{32} & a_{33} \end{vmatrix} = a_{11} \begin{vmatrix} a_{22} & a_{23} \\ a_{32} & a_{33} \end{vmatrix} - a_{12} \begin{vmatrix} a_{21} & a_{23} \\ a_{31} & a_{33} \end{vmatrix} + a_{13} \begin{vmatrix} a_{21} & a_{22} \\ a_{31} & a_{32} \end{vmatrix}$$

$$n \times n : \Delta = \begin{vmatrix} a_{11} & a_{12} & \cdots & a_{1n} \\ a_{21} & a_{22} & \cdots & a_{2n} \\ \vdots & \vdots & & \vdots \\ a_{n1} & a_{n2} & \cdots & a_{nn} \end{vmatrix}$$

The *minor*, α_{ij}, of the element a_{ij} is the $(n-1)$th order determinant formed from Δ by omitting the row and the column containing a_{ij}.

The *cofactor*, A_{ij}, of the element a_{ij} is given by $A_{ij} = (-1)^{i+j} \alpha_{ij}$.
The value of the $n \times n$ determinant is

$$\begin{aligned} \Delta &= a_{i1}A_{i1} + a_{i2}A_{i2} + \ldots + a_{in}A_{in} \text{(expansion by ith row)} \\ &= a_{1j}A_{1j} + a_{2j}A_{2j} + \ldots + a_{nj}A_{nj} \text{(expansion by jth column)} \\ & \quad \text{valid for } i, j = 1 \text{ to } n. \end{aligned}$$

Properties

1. The value of the determinant is unchanged if its rows and columns are interchanged.

2. The value of a determinant is unchanged if a multiple of any row (or column) is added to any other row (or column).

3. If the elements of two rows (or columns) are proportional, *i.e.* linearly dependent, then the value of the determinant is zero.

10

4. If the elements of two rows (or columns) are interchanged then the resulting determinant has the same numerical value but its sign is changed.

5. If the elements of a row (or column) are all multiplied by a constant k, then the value of the determinant is also multiplied by k.

Cramer's rule (efficient for only two equations in two unknowns or three equations in three unknowns).

$$
\begin{aligned}
a_{11}x_1 + a_{12}x_2 + a_{13}x_3 &= h_1 \\
a_{21}x_1 + a_{22}x_2 + a_{23}x_3 &= h_2 \\
a_{31}x_1 + a_{32}x_2 + a_{33}x_3 &= h_3
\end{aligned}
\qquad
\Delta = \begin{vmatrix} a_{11} & a_{12} & a_{13} \\ a_{21} & a_{22} & a_{23} \\ a_{31} & a_{32} & a_{33} \end{vmatrix}
$$

$$
\Delta_1 = \begin{vmatrix} h_1 & a_{12} & a_{13} \\ h_2 & a_{22} & a_{23} \\ h_3 & a_{32} & a_{33} \end{vmatrix}, \quad
\Delta_2 = \begin{vmatrix} a_{11} & h_1 & a_{13} \\ a_{21} & h_2 & a_{23} \\ a_{31} & h_3 & a_{33} \end{vmatrix}, \quad
\Delta_3 = \begin{vmatrix} a_{11} & a_{12} & h_1 \\ a_{21} & a_{22} & h_2 \\ a_{31} & a_{32} & h_3 \end{vmatrix}
$$

The solution is

$$
x_1 = \Delta_1/\Delta, \quad x_2 = \Delta_2/\Delta, \quad x_3 = \Delta_3/\Delta
$$

2.2 Matrices

The $m \times n$ matrix is written as

$$
\mathbf{A} = \begin{bmatrix}
a_{11} & a_{12} & \cdots & a_{1n} \\
a_{21} & a_{22} & \cdots & a_{2n} \\
\vdots & \vdots & & \vdots \\
a_{m1} & a_{m2} & \cdots & a_{mn}
\end{bmatrix}
$$

or $\mathbf{A} = [a_{ij}]$

Transpose matrix $\mathbf{A}^T = [a_{ji}]$ is $n \times m$

$\mathbf{A}$ is called a *symmetric matrix* if $\mathbf{A}^T = \mathbf{A}$

If $\mathbf{A}$ and $\mathbf{B}$ are of the same order then $\alpha\mathbf{A} + \beta\mathbf{B} = [\alpha a_{ij} + \beta b_{ij}]$

If $\mathbf{A}$ is $m \times r$ and $\mathbf{B}$ is $r \times n$ then

$$
\mathbf{AB} = \left[\sum_{k=1}^{r} a_{ik}b_{kj} \right] \text{ is } m \times n
$$

Unit matrix or *identity matrix* $\mathbf{I} = [\delta_{ij}]$ where the *Kronecker* δ is given by

$$
\delta_{ij} = \begin{cases} 0, & i \neq j \\ 1, & i = j \end{cases}
$$

11

Null matrix or *zero matrix* $\mathbf{0} = [0]$

For a square matrix $\mathbf{A}$ if $\det \mathbf{A} \neq 0$ then the *inverse matrix*, $\mathbf{A}^{-1}$, exists and is given by $\mathbf{A}^{-1} = \frac{1}{\det \mathbf{A}} \text{adj} \, \mathbf{A}$, where adj $\mathbf{A}$ is the transposed matrix of cofactors.

The inverse matrix has the property $\mathbf{A}\mathbf{A}^{-1} = \mathbf{A}^{-1}\mathbf{A} = \mathbf{I}$

If $\det \mathbf{A} = 0$ then $\mathbf{A}$ is said to be *singular.*

$\mathbf{A}$ is called an *orthogonal matrix* if $\mathbf{A}^T = \mathbf{A}^{-1}$

For a 2×2 matrix

$$\begin{bmatrix} a & b \\ c & d \end{bmatrix}^{-1} = \frac{1}{ad - bc} \begin{bmatrix} d & -b \\ -c & a \end{bmatrix}$$

For an $n \times n$ matrix

$$\det \mathbf{A} = \det \mathbf{A}^T \text{ and } \det(k\mathbf{A}) = k^n \det \mathbf{A}$$

The *rank* of a matrix, $\mathbf{A}$, is the largest non-zero sub-determinant of $\mathbf{A}$.

A set of vectors $\{\mathbf{v}_1, \mathbf{v}_2, \ldots, \mathbf{v}_n\}$ for a finite dimensional space is said to be *linearly dependent* if there exist scalars $\alpha_1, \alpha_2, \ldots, \alpha_n$, not all zero such that

$$\alpha_1 \mathbf{v}_1 + \alpha_2 \mathbf{v}_2 + \ldots + \alpha_n \mathbf{v}_n = \mathbf{0}$$

otherwise the set is *linearly independent.*

Suppose that $\{\mathbf{v}_1, \mathbf{v}_2, \ldots, \mathbf{v}_n\}$ is an arbitrary basis for a finite dimensional inner product space. Then the orthogonal basis $\{\mathbf{w}_1, \mathbf{w}_2, \ldots, \mathbf{w}_n\}$ may be obtained by the *Gram Schmidt process*

$$\mathbf{w}_n = \mathbf{v}_n - \frac{<\mathbf{v}_n, \mathbf{w}_1>}{||\mathbf{w}_1||^2}\mathbf{w}_1 - \frac{<\mathbf{v}_n, \mathbf{w}_2>}{||\mathbf{w}_2||^2}\mathbf{w}_2 -, \ldots, - \frac{<\mathbf{v}_n, \mathbf{w}_{n-1}>}{||\mathbf{w}_{n-1}||^2}\mathbf{w}_{n-1}$$

2.3 Systems of equations

For a system of m linear equations in n unknowns we write in matrix form

$$\mathbf{A}\mathbf{x} = \mathbf{b}$$

The explicit form is

$$
\begin{array}{ccccc}
a_{11}x_1 + a_{12}x_2 + & \cdots & +a_{1n}x_n & = & b_1 \\
a_{21}x_1 + a_{22}x_2 + & \cdots & +a_{2n}x_n & = & b_2 \\
& \vdots & & & \\
a_{m1}x_1 + a_{m2}x_2 + & \cdots & +a_{mn}x_n & = & b_m
\end{array}
$$

1. If rank $[\mathbf{A},\mathbf{b}] > \text{rank} \mathbf{A}$ then there is no solution.

2. If rank $[\mathbf{A},\mathbf{b}] = \text{rank} \mathbf{A} = n$ then there is a unique solution.

   In the case $m = n$, the solution is given by $\mathbf{x} = \mathbf{A}^{-1}\mathbf{b}$.

3. If rank $[\mathbf{A},\mathbf{b}] = \text{rank}\mathbf{A} < n$ then there is an infinite number of solutions.

It follows from 2. and 3. that, for a square matrix $\mathbf{A}$, the homogeneous set of equations $\mathbf{A}\mathbf{x} = \mathbf{0}$ has a non-trivial solution if and only if $\det\mathbf{A} = 0$.

2.4 Eigenvalues and eigenvectors

For a square matrix $\mathbf{A}$, the eigenvalues λ_i and corresponding eigenvectors $\mathbf{x}_i$ are given by

$$\mathbf{A}\mathbf{x}_i = \lambda_i\mathbf{x}_i$$

Thus the eigenvalues satisfy $\det[\mathbf{A} - \lambda\mathbf{I}] = 0$

Properties

Matrix	$p\mathbf{A}$	$\mathbf{A}^T$	$\mathbf{A}^{-1}$	$\mathbf{A}^k$	$\mathbf{A}+q\mathbf{I}$	$[\mathbf{A}+p\mathbf{I}]^{-1}$
Eigenvalues	$p\lambda_i$	λ_i	$1/\lambda_i$	λ_i^k	λ_i+q	$1/(\lambda_i+p)$

In each case the corresponding eigenvectors are $\mathbf{x}_i$.

The *trace* of the matrix $\mathbf{A}$, is given by

$$\text{tr}\mathbf{A} = a_{11} + a_{22} + \ldots + a_{nn}$$

$$\sum \lambda_i = \text{tr}\mathbf{A}, \qquad \prod \lambda_i = \det \mathbf{A}$$

Suppose that λ is an eigenvalue of $\mathbf{A}$ then $\lambda = 0$ iff $\det \mathbf{A} = 0$.

Chapter 3

Vector Algebra

3.1   Vector addition

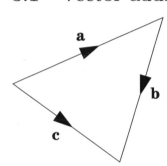

Triangle law $\mathbf{a} + \mathbf{b} = \mathbf{c}$

Component form $\mathbf{a} + \mathbf{b} = (a_1 + b_1)\,\hat{\mathbf{i}} + (a_2 + b_2)\,\hat{\mathbf{j}} + (a_3 + b_3)\,\hat{\mathbf{k}}$

3.2   Vector products

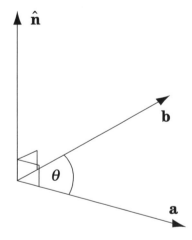

θ is the angle between the two vectors $\mathbf{a}$ and $\mathbf{b}$, $\hat{\mathbf{n}}$ is the unit vector perpendicular to both $\mathbf{a}$ and $\mathbf{b}$ in the sense that $\mathbf{a}$, $\mathbf{b}$ and $\hat{\mathbf{n}}$, in that order, form a right-handed system.

$$\mathbf{a}.\mathbf{b} = ab\cos\theta = \mathbf{b}.\mathbf{a}, \quad \mathbf{a}\times\mathbf{b} = ab\sin\theta\,\hat{\mathbf{n}}$$

In component form

$$\mathbf{a} = a_1\hat{\mathbf{i}} + a_2\hat{\mathbf{j}} + a_3\hat{\mathbf{k}}, \quad \mathbf{b} = b_1\hat{\mathbf{i}} + b_2\hat{\mathbf{j}} + b_3\hat{\mathbf{k}}$$

$$\mathbf{a.b} = a_1b_1 + a_2b_2 + a_3b_3$$

$$\mathbf{a} \times \mathbf{b} = \begin{vmatrix} \hat{\mathbf{i}} & \hat{\mathbf{j}} & \hat{\mathbf{k}} \\ a_1 & a_2 & a_3 \\ b_1 & b_2 & b_3 \end{vmatrix} = -\mathbf{b} \times \mathbf{a}$$

Magnitude: $|\mathbf{a}| = a = \sqrt{a_1^2 + a_2^2 + a_3^2}$

Unit vector in the direction of the vector $\mathbf{a}$ is $\hat{\mathbf{a}} = \dfrac{1}{|\mathbf{a}|}\mathbf{a} =$

$$\mathbf{a.(b \times c)} = \mathbf{(a \times b).c} = \begin{vmatrix} a_1 & a_2 & a_3 \\ b_1 & b_2 & b_3 \\ c_1 & c_2 & c_3 \end{vmatrix} = [\mathbf{a\ b\ c}]$$

$$\mathbf{a} \times (\mathbf{b \times c}) = (\mathbf{a.c})\,\mathbf{b} - (\mathbf{a.b})\,\mathbf{c}$$

$$(\mathbf{a \times b}) \times \mathbf{c} = (\mathbf{a.c})\,\mathbf{b} - (\mathbf{b.c})\,\mathbf{a}$$

$$(\mathbf{a \times b}).(\mathbf{c \times d}) = \begin{vmatrix} \mathbf{a.c} & \mathbf{a.d} \\ \mathbf{b.c} & \mathbf{b.d} \end{vmatrix}$$

$$(\mathbf{a \times b}) \times (\mathbf{c \times d}) = [\mathbf{a\ b\ c}]\,\mathbf{c} - [\mathbf{a\ b\ c}]\,\mathbf{d}$$

3.3 Polar coordinates in two and three dimensions

Plane polar coordinates (r, θ)

$$x = r\cos\theta, \quad y = r\sin\theta$$

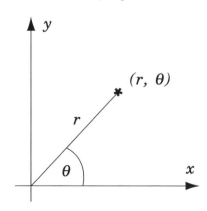

Cylindrical polar coordinates (R, ϕ, z)

$$x = R\cos\phi, \quad y = R\sin\phi$$

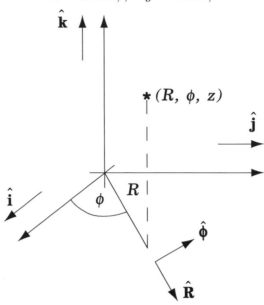

Unit vectors $\left(\hat{\mathbf{R}}, \hat{\boldsymbol{\phi}}, \hat{\mathbf{k}}\right)$ form a right-handed system.
Relationships with Cartesian unit vectors:

$$\hat{\mathbf{R}} = \cos\phi\,\hat{\mathbf{i}} + \sin\phi\,\hat{\mathbf{j}}, \quad \hat{\boldsymbol{\phi}} = -\sin\phi\,\hat{\mathbf{i}} + \cos\phi\,\hat{\mathbf{j}}$$

Spherical polar coordinates (r, θ, ϕ)

$$x = r\sin\theta\cos\phi, \quad y = r\sin\theta\sin\phi, \quad z = r\cos\theta$$

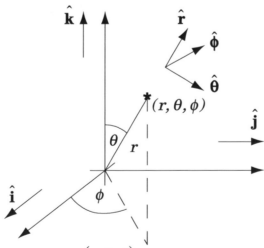

Unit vectors $\left(\hat{\mathbf{r}}, \hat{\boldsymbol{\theta}}, \hat{\boldsymbol{\phi}}\right)$ form a right-handed system.
Relationship with cylindrical unit vectors:

$$\hat{\mathbf{r}} = \sin\theta\,\hat{\mathbf{R}} + \cos\theta\,\hat{\mathbf{k}}, \quad \hat{\boldsymbol{\theta}} = -\cos\theta\,\hat{\mathbf{R}} + \sin\theta\,\hat{\mathbf{k}}$$

16

Chapter 4

Calculus

4.1 Rules for manipulation of derivatives and integrals

Differentiation

Linearity rule $\dfrac{d}{dx}(au + bv) = a\dfrac{du}{dx} + b\dfrac{dv}{dx}$

Product rule $\dfrac{d}{dx}(uv) = \dfrac{du}{dx}v + u\dfrac{dv}{dx}$

Quotient rule $\dfrac{d}{dx}\left(\dfrac{u}{v}\right) = \left(v\dfrac{du}{dx} - u\dfrac{dv}{dx}\right)/v^2$

Leibniz rule

$$
\begin{aligned}
D^n(uv) &= uD^n v + \binom{n}{1}(Du)\,D^{n-1}v + \binom{n}{2}(Du)\,D^{n-2}v + \ldots + (D^n u)\,v \\
&= \sum_{r=0}^{n}\binom{n}{r}(D^r u)\,D^{n-r}v, \text{ where } D \equiv \dfrac{d}{dx}
\end{aligned}
$$

Chain rule for ordinary differentiation (function of a function rule)
Leibniz notation

$$y = y(x) \text{ and } x = x(u);$$

$$\frac{dy}{du} = \frac{dy}{dx}\frac{dx}{du}$$

Function notation

$$[F(g(x))]' = F'(g(x))\,g'(x)$$

Chain rule for partial differentiation

$$F(u, v) = f(x, y) \text{ with } x = x(u, v), y = y(u, v)$$

$$\frac{\partial F}{\partial u} = \frac{\partial f}{\partial x}\frac{\partial x}{\partial u} + \frac{\partial f}{\partial y}\frac{\partial y}{\partial u}; \qquad \frac{\partial F}{\partial v} = \frac{\partial f}{\partial x}\frac{\partial x}{\partial v} + \frac{\partial f}{\partial y}\frac{\partial y}{\partial v}$$

17

Total differential

$$df = \frac{\partial f}{\partial x}dx + \frac{\partial f}{\partial y}dy$$

Integration
Integration by parts

$$\int u\frac{dv}{dx}dx = uv - \int v\frac{du}{dx}dx$$

Integration by substitution

$$\int f\left(x\right)dx = \int F\left(u\right)\frac{dx}{du}du \text{ where } F\left(u\right) = f\left(x\left(u\right)\right)$$

$$\int \frac{f'\left(x\right)}{f\left(x\right)}dx = \ln|f(x)|$$

$$\int f'\left(x\right)\left[f\left(x\right)\right]^n dx = \frac{\left[f\left(x\right)\right]^{n+1}}{n+1}, \qquad n \neq -1$$

Differentiation of integrals

If $\quad I\left(x\right) = \int_{u(x)}^{v(x)} F(x,t)dt, \;$ then

$$\frac{dI}{dx} = F(x,v(x))\frac{dv}{dx} - F(x,u(x))\frac{du}{dx} + \int_{u(x)}^{v(x)} \frac{\partial F}{\partial x}(x,t)dt$$

4.2   Standard derivatives and integrals

Table of derivatives and integrals 1

$$df/dx \qquad f(x) \qquad F(x) = \int f(x)dx$$

(add arbitrary constant where necessary)

nx^{n-1}	x^n	$\dfrac{x^{n+1}}{n+1}(n \neq -1)$ (4.1)
$-\dfrac{1}{x^2}$	$\dfrac{1}{x}$	$\ln|x|$ (4.2)
e^x	e^x	e^x (4.3)
$a^x \ln a$	a^x	$\dfrac{a^x}{\ln a}$ (4.4)
$\dfrac{1}{x}$	$\ln x$	$x(\ln x - 1)$ (4.5)
$\dfrac{1}{x \ln b}$	$\log_b x$	$x(\log_b x - \log_b e)$ (4.6)
$\cos x$	$\sin x$	$-\cos x$ (4.7)
$-\sin x$	$\cos x$	$\sin x$ (4.8)
$\sec^2 x$	$\tan x$	$\ln|\sec x|$ (4.9)
$\sec x \tan x$	$\sec x$	$\begin{cases} \ln|\sec x + \tan x| \\ \ln|\tan(x/2 + \pi/4)| \end{cases}$ (4.10)
$-\mathrm{cosec}x \cot x$	$\mathrm{cosec}x$	$\begin{cases} \ln|\mathrm{cosec}x - \cot x| \\ \ln|\tan(x/2)| \end{cases}$ (4.11)
$-\mathrm{cosec}^2 x$	$\cot x$	$\ln|\sin x|$ (4.12)
$\dfrac{1}{\sqrt{1-x^2}}$	$\sin^{-1} x$	$x\sin^{-1} x + \sqrt{1-x^2}$ (4.13)
$\dfrac{-1}{\sqrt{1-x^2}}$	$\cos^{-1} x$	$x\cos^{-1} x - \sqrt{1-x^2}$ (4.14)
$\dfrac{1}{1+x^2}$	$\tan^{-1} x$	$x\tan^{-1} x - \dfrac{1}{2}\ln(1+x^2)$ (4.15)
$\cosh x$	$\sinh x$	$\cosh x$ (4.16)
$\sinh x$	$\cosh x$	$\sinh x$ (4.17)
$\mathrm{sech}^2 x$	$\tanh x$	$\begin{cases} \ln\cosh x \\ \ln(e^x + e^{-x}) \end{cases}$ (4.18)

continued. . .

Table of derivatives and integrals 2

df/dx	$f(x)$	$F(x) = \int f(x)dx$	
		(add arbitrary constant where necessary)	
$-\operatorname{sech}x \tanh x$	$\operatorname{sech}x$	$\begin{cases} 2\tan^{-1}(\tanh x/2) \\ 2\tan^{-1}e^x \\ \tan^{-1}(\sinh x) \end{cases}$	(4.19)
$-\operatorname{cosech}x \coth x$	$\operatorname{cosech}x$	$\begin{cases} \ln|\tanh(x/2)| \\ -\ln|\operatorname{cosech}x + \coth x| \\ \ln|(e^x - 1)/(e^x + 1)| \end{cases}$	(4.20)
$-\operatorname{cosech}^2 x$	$\coth x$	$\begin{cases} \ln|\sinh x| \\ \ln|e^x - e^{-x}| \end{cases}$	(4.21)
$\dfrac{1}{\sqrt{1+x^2}}$	$\sinh^{-1}x$	$x\sinh^{-1}x - \sqrt{1+x^2}$	(4.22)
$\dfrac{1}{\sqrt{x^2-1}}$	$\cosh^{-1}x$	$x\cosh^{-1}x - \sqrt{x^2-1}$	(4.23)
$\dfrac{1}{1-x^2}$	$\tanh^{-1}x$	$x\tanh^{-1}x - \dfrac{1}{2}\ln(1-x^2)$	(4.24)
$\dfrac{x}{(a^2-x^2)^{\frac{3}{2}}}$	$\dfrac{1}{\sqrt{a^2-x^2}}$	$\begin{cases} \sin^{-1}\dfrac{x}{a} \\ -\cos^{-1}\dfrac{x}{a} \end{cases}$	(4.25)
$\dfrac{-2x}{(x^2+a^2)^2}$	$\dfrac{1}{x^2+a^2}$	$\dfrac{1}{a}\tan^{-1}\dfrac{x}{a}$	(4.26)
$\dfrac{a^2-2x^2}{x^2(x^2-a^2)^{\frac{3}{2}}}$	$\dfrac{1}{x\sqrt{x^2-a^2}}$	$\dfrac{1}{a}\sec^{-1}\dfrac{x}{a}$	(4.27)
$\dfrac{-x}{(a^2+x^2)^{\frac{3}{2}}}$	$\dfrac{1}{\sqrt{a^2+x^2}}$	$\begin{cases} \sinh^{-1}\dfrac{x}{a} \\ \ln|x + \sqrt{x^2+a^2}| \end{cases}$	(4.28)
$\dfrac{-x}{(x^2-a^2)^{\frac{3}{2}}}$	$\dfrac{1}{\sqrt{x^2-a^2}}$	$\begin{cases} \cosh^{-1}\dfrac{x}{a} \\ \ln|x + \sqrt{x^2-a^2}| \end{cases}$	(4.29)
$\dfrac{2x}{(a^2-x^2)^2}$	$\dfrac{1}{(a^2-x^2)}$	$\begin{cases} \dfrac{1}{a}\tanh^{-1}\dfrac{x}{a} \\ \dfrac{1}{2a}\ln\left|\dfrac{a+x}{a-x}\right| \end{cases}$	(4.30)

continued...

$$df/dx \qquad f(x) \qquad F(x) = \int f(x)dx$$

(add arbitrary constant where necessary)

$$\frac{x}{\sqrt{x^2 \pm a^2}} \qquad \sqrt{x^2 \pm a^2} \qquad \frac{x}{2}\sqrt{x^2 \pm a^2} \pm \frac{a^2}{2}\ln|x + \sqrt{x^2 \pm a^2}| \quad (4.31)$$

$$\frac{-x}{\sqrt{a^2 - x^2}} \qquad \sqrt{a^2 - x^2} \qquad \frac{x}{2}\sqrt{a^2 - x^2} + \frac{a^2}{2}\sin^{-1}\frac{x}{a} \qquad (4.32)$$

$$e^{ax}(a\cos bx - b\sin bx) \quad e^{ax}\cos bx \qquad \frac{e^{ax}}{a^2 + b^2}(a\cos bx + b\sin bx) \qquad (4.33)$$

$$e^{ax}(a\sin bx + b\cos bx) \quad e^{ax}\sin bx \qquad \frac{e^{ax}}{a^2 + b^2}(a\sin bx - b\cos bx) \qquad (4.34)$$

4.3 Definite integrals

Wallis's formulae (reduction formulae also hold if upper limit is π or 2π.)

$$S_n = \int_0^{\frac{\pi}{2}} \sin^n \theta d\theta = \frac{n-1}{n} S_{n-2}$$

$$C_n = \int_0^{\frac{\pi}{2}} \cos^n \theta d\theta = \frac{n-1}{n} C_{n-2}.$$

$$I_{m,n} = \int_0^{\frac{\pi}{2}} \sin^m \theta \cos^n \theta d\theta = \frac{m-1}{m+n} I_{m-2,n} = \frac{n-1}{m+n} I_{m,n-2}.$$

$$S_n = C_n = \frac{(n-1)(n-3)(n-5)\ldots}{n(n-2)(n-4)\ldots}p;$$

$$I_{m,n} = \frac{(m-1)(m-3)\ldots(n-1)(n-3)\ldots}{(m+n)(m+n-2)(m+n-4)\ldots}q;$$

where $p = \begin{cases} \frac{\pi}{2} & n \text{ even} \\ 1 & n \text{ odd} \end{cases} \qquad q = \begin{cases} \frac{\pi}{2} & \text{both } m \text{ and } n \text{ even} \\ 1 & \text{otherwise} \end{cases}$

For all integer values of m and n:

$$\int_{-\pi}^{\pi} \sin m\theta \cos n\theta d\theta = 0$$

$$\int_{-\pi}^{\pi} \sin m\theta \sin n\theta d\theta = \int_{-\pi}^{\pi} \cos m\theta \cos n\theta d\theta = \pi\delta_{mn}, \qquad m, n \neq 0$$

(δ_{mn} is the Kronecker δ see page 11)

$$\int_{-\infty}^{\infty} e^{-x^2}\,dx = \sqrt{\pi}; \qquad\qquad \int_{-\infty}^{\infty} e^{-(ax^2+bx)}\,dx = \sqrt{\frac{\pi}{a}}\exp(b^2/4a) \qquad a > 0$$

$$\int_{-\infty}^{\infty} \frac{\cos ax}{1+x^2}\,dx = \pi e^{-|a|}; \qquad \int_{-\infty}^{\infty} \frac{\sin ax}{1+x^2}\,dx = 0$$

Error function

$$\mathrm{erf}(x) = \frac{2}{\sqrt{\pi}}\int_0^x e^{-t^2}\,dt$$

Complementary error function

$$\mathrm{erfc}(x) = 1 - \mathrm{erf}(x) = \frac{2}{\sqrt{\pi}}\int_x^{\infty} e^{-t^2}\,dt$$

$$\mathrm{erf}(0) = \mathrm{erfc}(\infty) = 0, \quad \mathrm{erf}(\infty) = \mathrm{erfc}(0) = 1$$

For the *Chebyshev polynomials* $T_n(x)$, $T_m(x)$ (see page 57)

$$\int_{-1}^{1} \frac{T_n(x)T_m(x)}{\sqrt{1-x^2}}\,dx = \begin{cases} 0 & n \neq m \\ \pi & n = m = 0 \\ \pi/2 & n = m \neq 0 \end{cases}$$

Gamma function

$$\Gamma(t) = \int_0^{\infty} e^{-x}x^{t-1}\,dx \qquad t \neq 0, -1, -2, \ldots$$
$$\Gamma(t) = (t-1)\Gamma(t-1)$$
$$\quad = (t-1)(t-2)(t-3)\ldots\Gamma(t-[t])$$
$$\Gamma(\tfrac{1}{2}) = \sqrt{\pi}$$
$$\Gamma(n+1) = n! \text{ when } n \text{ is an integer}$$

Beta function

$$B(s,t) = \int_0^1 x^{s-1}(1-x)^{t-1}\,dx = \Gamma(s)\Gamma(t)/\Gamma(s+t)$$

Legendre polynomial

$$P_n(x) = \frac{1}{2\pi}\int_0^{2\pi} [x + \sqrt{x^2-1}\cos\theta]^n\,d\theta = \frac{1}{2^n n!}\frac{d^n}{dx^n}\left(x^2-1\right)^n$$

$$P_0(x) = 1, \quad P_1(x) = x, \quad P_2(x) = (3x^2-1)/2, \quad P_3(x) = (5x^3-3x)/2, \ldots$$

Generating function

$$(1 - 2xh + h^2)^{-\frac{1}{2}} = \sum_{n=0}^{\infty} P_n(x)h^n$$

$P_n(x)$ is a solution of *Legendre's equation* $(1-x^2)y'' - 2xy' + n(n+1)y = 0$. A second, linearly independent, solution is the *Legendre function* of the second kind $Q_n(x)$ which is not a polynomial.

Bessel function

$$J_n(x) = \frac{x^n}{2^{n-1}\sqrt{\pi}\Gamma(n+\frac{1}{2})} \int_0^{\frac{\pi}{2}} \cos(x\sin\theta)\cos^{2n}\theta\, d\theta.$$

$J_n(x)$ is a solution of *Bessel's equation* $x^2y'' + xy' + (x^2 - n^2)y = 0$
A second, linearly independent, solution, $Y_n(x)$, is the Bessel function of the second kind.
The *modified Bessel function*, $I_n(x)$, satisfies the equation
$x^2y'' + xy' - (x^2 + n^2)y = 0$ and a second linearly independent solution is $K_n(x)$, the modified Bessel function of the second kind.

4.4 Radius of curvature of a curve

Intrinsic coordinates: $\rho = \dfrac{ds}{d\psi}$.   Curvature: $\kappa = \dfrac{1}{\rho}$.

Cartesian coordinates: $\rho = \dfrac{[1 + (y')^2]^{3/2}}{|y''|}$.

Parametric coordinates: $\rho = \dfrac{((\dot{x})^2 + (\dot{y})^2)^{3/2}}{|\dot{x}\ddot{y} - \ddot{x}\dot{y}|}$

4.5 Stationary points

Functions of one variable
The function $f(x)$ has stationary points given by $f'(x) = 0$. The stationary point, $(x_0, f(x_0))$, is a local *maximum* if $f''(x_0) < 0$ or a local *minimum* if $f''(x_0) > 0$. If $f''(x_0) = 0$ then the second derivative test is inconclusive and we consider the sign of $f'(x \pm \epsilon)$ where ϵ is small and positive. If $f''(x_0) = 0$ and $f'(x_0 \pm \epsilon)$ are both positive or both negative then x_0 is a *point of inflection*.

Functions of more than one variable
Stationary points occur when the first partial derivatives vanish. For a function of two variables, $f(x, y)$, stationary points are given by $f_x = f_y = 0$. The Hessian is given by

$$H(x, y) = \begin{vmatrix} f_{xx} & f_{xy} \\ f_{yx} & f_{yy} \end{vmatrix}$$

The stationary point is:
a *maximum* if $f_{xx} < 0$, $f_{yy} < 0$ and $H > 0$,

a *minimum* if $f_{xx} > 0, f_{yy} > 0$ and $H > 0$,
a *saddle point* if $H < 0$.

Lagrange multipliers
To find the stationary point of $f(x, y)$ subject to the constraint $g(x, y) = 0$, find the stationary points of the function

$$\phi(x, y; \lambda) = f(x, y) + \lambda g(x, y).$$

4.6   Limits and series

$$\lim_{x \to 0} \frac{\sin x}{x} = 1, \quad \lim_{x \to 0} \frac{\tan x}{x} = 1, \quad \lim_{n \to \infty} \left(1 + \frac{x}{n}\right)^n = e^x.$$

$$\lim_{x \to 0} x^\alpha \ln x = 0, \quad \lim_{x \to \infty} x^{-\alpha} \ln x = 0, \quad \lim_{x \to \infty} x^\alpha e^{-x} = 0, \quad \text{(in all cases } \alpha > 0\text{)}.$$

De L'Hôpital's rule

If $f(a) = g(a) = 0$, then $\lim\limits_{x \to a} \dfrac{f(x)}{g(x)} = \lim\limits_{x \to a} \dfrac{f'(x)}{g'(x)}$, provided $g'(a) \neq 0$.

Taylor's theorem

$$f(x) = f(a) + (x-a)f'(a) + \frac{(x-a)^2}{2!}f''(a) + \ldots + \frac{(x-a)^n}{n!}f^{(n)}(a) + \epsilon_n$$

where $\epsilon_n = \dfrac{(x-a)^{n+1}}{(n+1)!} f^{(n+1)}(c)$ for some $c \in (a, x)$.

Taylor's series for a function of one variable

$$f(x) = f(a) + (x-a)f'(a) + \frac{(x-a)^2}{2!}f''(a) + \ldots + \frac{(x-a)^n}{n!}f^{(n)}(a),$$

or, writing $x = a + h$,

$$f(a+h) = f(a) + hf'(a) + \frac{h^2}{2!}f''(a) + \ldots + \frac{h^n}{n!}f^{(n)}(a) + \ldots$$

Maclaurin series (put $a = 0, h = x$ in Taylor's series)

$$f(x) = f(0) + xf'(0) + \frac{x^2}{2!}f''(0) + \ldots + \frac{x^n}{n!}f^{(n)}(0) + \ldots$$

Power series

If the power series $a_0 + a_1 x + a_2 x^2 + \ldots + a_n x^n + \ldots = \sum\limits_{n=0}^{\infty} a_n x^n$ is convergent for $|x| < R$ then R is called the *radius of convergence* of the series.

$$R = \lim_{n \to \infty} \frac{|a_{n+1}|}{|a_n|}$$

Some useful series:

$$\ln(1+x) = x - \frac{x^2}{2} + \frac{x^3}{3} - \frac{x^4}{4} + \ldots + (-1)^{n+1}\frac{x^n}{n} + \ldots, \quad -1 < x \le 1$$

$$\ln(1-x) = -x - \frac{x^2}{2} - \frac{x^3}{3} - \frac{x^4}{4} - \ldots - \frac{x^n}{n} - \ldots, \quad -1 < x \le 1$$

$$(1 \pm x)^n = 1 \pm nx + \frac{n(n-1)}{2!}x^2 \pm \frac{n(n-1)(n-2)}{3!}x^3 + \ldots \quad -1 < x < 1$$

[This is the *binomial series*. If n is a positive integer the series terminates after $n+1$ terms, otherwise it converges if and only if $|x| < 1$.]

$$(1 \mp x)^{-1} = 1 \pm x + x^2 \pm x^3 + \ldots + x^{2n} \pm x^{2n+1} + \ldots, \quad |x| < 1$$

$$e^x = 1 + x + \frac{x^2}{2!} + \frac{x^3}{3!} + \frac{x^4}{4!} + \ldots + \frac{x^n}{n!} + \ldots, \quad \text{all } x$$

$$\sin x = x - \frac{x^3}{3!} + \frac{x^5}{5!} - \frac{x^7}{7!} + \ldots + \frac{(-1)^n x^{2n+1}}{(2n+1)!} + \ldots, \quad \text{all } x$$

$$\cos x = 1 - \frac{x^2}{2!} + \frac{x^4}{4!} - \frac{x^6}{6!} + \ldots + \frac{(-1)^n x^{2n}}{(2n)!} + \ldots, \quad \text{all } x$$

$$\tan x = x + \frac{x^3}{3} + \frac{2x^5}{15} + \frac{x^7}{315} + \ldots, \quad |x| < \frac{\pi}{2}$$

$$\sin^{-1} x = \frac{\pi}{2} - \cos^{-1} x$$

$$= x + \frac{x^3}{6} + \frac{3x^5}{40} + \frac{5x^7}{112} + \ldots + \frac{(2n)!}{2^{2n}(n!)^2}\frac{x^{2n+1}}{(2n+1)} + \ldots, \quad |x| < 1$$

$$\tan^{-1} x = x - \frac{x^3}{3} + \frac{x^5}{5} + \ldots + (-1)^{n+1}\frac{x^{2n+1}}{(2n+1)} + \ldots, \quad |x| < 1$$

To obtain the series for the corresponding hyperbolic functions, see the note following Osborne's rule on page 5.

Taylor's series for a function of two variables

$$f(a+h, b+k) = f(a,b) + \{hf_x(a+b) + kf_y(a,b)\}$$
$$+ \frac{1}{2!}\{h^2 f_{xx}(a,b) + 2hk f_{xy}(a,b) + k^2 f_{yy}(a,b)\} + \ldots$$
$$= \sum_{n=0}^{\infty} \frac{1}{n!}\left(h\frac{\partial}{\partial x} + k\frac{\partial}{\partial y}\right)^n f(a,b)$$

4.7 Multiple integration

$$\int\int_R f(x,y)\,dx\,dy = \int\int_{R'} f(x(u,v), y(u,v))\left| J\left(\frac{x,y}{u,v}\right)\right|\,du\,dv$$

where the region R in the xy-plane is mapped to the region R' in the uv-plane and the *Jacobian* of the transformation is given by

$$J\left(\frac{x,y}{u,v}\right) = \begin{vmatrix} x_u & y_u \\ x_v & y_v \end{vmatrix}$$

Plane polar coordinates

$$J = r, \text{ so that } dA = dxdy = rdrd\theta$$

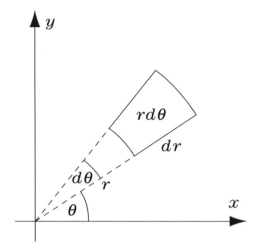

Volume and surface integrals
Cylindrical polar coordinates

$$dS = Rd\phi dz \text{ and } dV = RdRd\phi dz$$

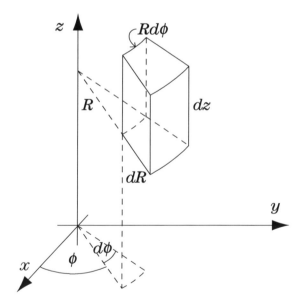

Spherical polar coordinates

$$dS = r^2 \sin\theta d\theta d\phi \text{ and } dV = r^2 \sin\theta dr d\theta d\phi$$

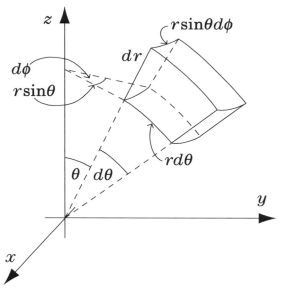

Line integrals
Green's theorem in the plane

$$\int_C (Pdx + Qdy) = \int\int_R \left(\frac{\partial Q}{\partial x} - \frac{\partial P}{\partial y}\right) dxdy$$

where C is the closed curve bounding the region R.

$\int_C (Pdx + Qdy)$ is independent of the path if and only if $\dfrac{\partial Q}{\partial x} = \dfrac{\partial P}{\partial y}$.

The line integral of $\mathbf{F}$ is independent of the path C joining A to B, if and only if there exists a potential function ϕ such that $\mathbf{F} = \text{grad}\phi$, or equivalently, if and only if $\text{curl}\mathbf{F} \equiv \mathbf{0}$. In this case

$$\int_{C_{AB}} \mathbf{F}.d\mathbf{s} = \int_A^B d\phi = \phi_B - \phi_A$$

4.8   Applications of integration

Arc length of a curve

Cartesian form: $\displaystyle\int_a^b \sqrt{1 + (y')^2}dx$

Polar form: $\displaystyle\int_{\theta_1}^{\theta_2} \sqrt{r^2 + (dr/d\theta)^2}d\theta$

Parametric form: $\displaystyle\int_{t_1}^{t_2} \sqrt{\dot{x}^2 + \dot{y}^2}dt$

Solid of revolution

The surface area of the solid of revolution obtained by one complete revolution of the curve $y = f(x)$ about the x-axis is given by

$$2\pi \int_a^b y\sqrt{1 + (y')^2}dx$$

The volume of the solid of revolution obtained by one complete revolution of the curve $y = f(x)$ about the x-axis is given by

$$\pi \int_a^b y^2 dx$$

Centroid

The centroid of the volume of the solid of revolution above is at $(\bar{x}, 0)$ where

$$\bar{x} = \int_a^b xy^2 dx \left/ \int_a^b y^2 dx \right.$$

The centroid of the area between the curve $y = f(x)$, the $x-$axis and the lines $x = a, x = b$ is given by

$$\bar{x} = \int_a^b xy\,dx \left/ \int_a^b y\,dx \right. , \quad \bar{y} = \int_a^b y^2 dx \left/ 2\int_a^b y\,dx \right.$$

Mean value

The mean value of $f(x)$ between $x = a, x = b$ is

$$\frac{1}{b-a} \int_a^b f(x)dx$$

Root mean square value

The *RMS* of the function $f(x)$ between $x = a, x = b$ is given by

$$\left(\frac{1}{b-a} \int_a^b [f(x)]^2\, dx \right)^{\frac{1}{2}}$$

Moments of area and inertia

The first and second moments of a plane area A about an axis are given respectively by

$$\int\int_A r\,dA \text{ and } \int\int_A r^2 dA$$

where r is the distance from the axis of the element dA.

The moment of inertia, I, of a body, of density ρ and volume V, about an axis is given by

$$\int_V r^2 \rho \, dV$$

where r is the distance from the axis of the element dV.

Parallel axes theorem

If I_G is the moment of inertia about an axis through the centroid and I is the moment of inertia about a parallel axis distance d away, then

$$I = I_G + md^2$$

Table of moments of inertia 1

Uniform Body mass m	Axis	M. of I.
1. Bar length $2a$	Perpendicular to bar through one end	$\dfrac{ma^2}{3}$
	Perpendicular to bar through centroid	$\dfrac{4ma^2}{3}$
2. Rectangular lamina sides $2a$ and $2b$	Parallel to side $2b$ through centroid	$\dfrac{ma^2}{3}$
	Perpendicular to plane through centroid	$\dfrac{m(a^2 + b^2)}{3}$
3. Rectangular solid edges $2a$ and $2b$, depth $2d$	Perpendicular to face $4ab$ through centroid	$\dfrac{m(a^2 + b^2)}{3}$
	Coinciding with edge $2d$	$\dfrac{4m(a^2 + b^2)}{3}$
4. Solid sphere radius r	Diameter	$\dfrac{2mr^2}{5}$
	Tangent	$\dfrac{7mr^2}{5}$
5. Spherical shell radii R and r	Diameter	$\dfrac{2m(R^5 - r^5)}{3(R^3 - r^3)}$
	Tangent	$\dfrac{m(7R^5 - 5R^2r^3 - 2r^5)}{5(R^3 - r^3)}$

continued...

Table of moments of inertia 2

Uniform Body mass m	Axis	M.of I.
6. Disc radius r	Diameter	$\dfrac{mr^2}{4}$
	Perpendicular to disc through centroid	$\dfrac{mr^2}{2}$
7. Annular ring radii R and r	Diameter	$\dfrac{m(R^2 + r^2)}{4}$
	Perpendicular to plane of ring through centroid	$\dfrac{m(R^2 + r^2)}{2}$
8. Solid cylinder radius r length $2a$	Axis	$\dfrac{mr^2}{2}$
	Perpendicular to axis through centroid	$m\left(\dfrac{a^2}{3} + \dfrac{r^2}{4}\right)$
9. Cylindrical shell radii R and r length $2a$	Axis	$\dfrac{m(R^2 + r^2)}{2}$
	Perpendicular to axis through centroid	$m\left(\dfrac{a^2}{3} + \dfrac{R^2 + r^2}{4}\right)$

For entries 2, 6 and 7 the second moment of-area J is given by $J = IA/m$ where A is the area.

4.9 Kinematics and dynamics

Kinematics

Position vector

$$\begin{aligned}\mathbf{r} &= x\mathbf{i} + y\mathbf{j} + z\mathbf{k} \quad \text{(Cartesian coordinates)} \\ &= r\hat{\mathbf{r}} \quad \text{(Plane polar coordinates)}\end{aligned}$$

Velocity vector

$$\begin{aligned}\dot{\mathbf{r}} &= \dot{x}\hat{\mathbf{i}} + \dot{y}\hat{\mathbf{j}} + \dot{z}\hat{\mathbf{k}} \quad \text{(Cartesian coordinates)} \\ &= \dot{r}\hat{\mathbf{r}} + r\dot{\theta}\hat{\boldsymbol{\theta}} \quad \text{(Plane polar coordinates)} \\ &= \dot{s}\hat{\mathbf{t}} \quad \text{(Intrinsic coordinates)}\end{aligned}$$

Acceleration vector

$$\begin{aligned}\ddot{\mathbf{r}} &= \ddot{x}\hat{\mathbf{i}} + \ddot{y}\hat{\mathbf{j}} + \ddot{z}\hat{\mathbf{k}} \quad &&\text{(Cartesian coordinates)} \\ &= (\ddot{r} - r\dot{\theta}^2)\hat{\mathbf{r}} + \frac{1}{r}\frac{d}{dt}(r^2\dot{\theta})\hat{\boldsymbol{\theta}} \quad &&\text{(Plane polar coordinates)} \\ &= \ddot{s}\hat{\mathbf{t}} + \frac{\dot{s}^2}{\rho}\hat{\mathbf{n}} \quad &&\text{(Intrinsic coordinates)}\end{aligned}$$

For uniform motion with angular velocity ω in a circle of radius a, speed is $v = a\omega$ and acceleration is $v^2/a = a\omega^2$ directed towards the centre.

Dynamics

Newton's second law for a particle of mass m moving under the influence of an external force $\mathbf{F}$

$$\mathbf{F} = m\ddot{\mathbf{r}}$$

For a rigid body moving about an axis with angular velocity ω and external torque Γ we have

$$\Gamma = I\dot{\omega}$$

where I is the moment of inertia about the axis.

Chapter 5

Ordinary Differential Equations

5.1   First order equations

$$\frac{dy}{dx} = F(x,y) \text{ or } y' = F(x,y)$$

Variables separable

$$\frac{dy}{dx} = f(x)g(y) \qquad (g(y) \neq 0)$$

General Solution is

$$\int \frac{1}{g(y)} dy = \int f(x)dx + \text{constant}$$

Linear equation *(integrating factor method)*

$$\frac{dy}{dx} + P(x)y = Q(x)$$

Integrating factor: $\mu(x) = \exp(\int P(x)dx)$

Then $\dfrac{d}{dx}(\mu(x)y) = \mu(x)Q(x)$ and the

General Solution is

$$\mu(x)y = \int \mu(x)Q(x)dx + \text{constant}$$

Initial-value problem

Find the general solution of

$$\frac{dy}{dx} = F(x,y) \quad \text{subject to } y(x_0) = y_0$$

i.e. solve the differential equation containing one arbitrary constant and determine the value of the constant to satisfy the *initial condition* that $y = y_0$ when $x = x_0$.

5.2   Second order equations

The general linear equation with constant coefficients

$$a\frac{d^2y}{dx^2} + b\frac{dy}{dx} + cy = f(x) \text{ or } ay'' + by' + cy = f(x)$$

Complementary function y_c
Solution of the associated homogeneous equation

$$ay'' + by' + cy = 0 \qquad (a, b, c \text{ real})$$

Auxiliary equation $a\lambda^2 + b\lambda + c = 0$
Three cases:
Two real distinct roots, λ_1, λ_2
Linearly independent solutions $e^{\lambda_1 x}$ and $e^{\lambda_2 x}$;

$$y_c = C_1 e^{\lambda_1 x} + C_2 e^{\lambda_2 x}$$

One real repeated root, λ_1
Linearly independent solutions $e^{\lambda_1 x}$ and $xe^{\lambda_1 x}$;

$$y_c = e^{\lambda_1 x}(C_1 + C_2 x)$$

Complex conjugate roots, $\alpha \pm j\beta$
Linearly independent solutions $e^{\alpha x}\cos\beta x$ and $e^{\alpha x}\sin\beta x$;

$$y_c = e^{\alpha x}(C_1 \cos\beta x + C_2 \sin\beta x)$$

Particular integral y_p
Any solution of the non-homogeneous equation

$$ay'' + by' + cy = f(x)$$

Method of undetermined coefficients
Choose a suitable *trial function* for y_p according to the right-hand-side, $f(x)$.

$f(x)$	trial function
constant	constant
$px + q$	$lx + m$
$px^2 + qx + r$	$lx^2 + mx + n$
polynomial degree n	$a_n x^n + a_{n-1}x^{n-1} + \ldots + a_1 x^1 + a_0$
$e^{\omega x}$	$ke^{\omega x}$
$p\cos\omega x$	$m\cos\omega x + n\sin\omega x$
$q\sin\omega x$	$m\cos\omega x + n\sin\omega x$
$\mathrm{Re}[(p - jq)e^{j\omega x}]$	$\mathrm{Re}[ze^{j\omega x}]$

Beware: If the *rhs* includes one of the complementary function linearly independent solutions then choose x times the appropriate trial function.

General Solution The sum of the complementary function and a particular integral $y = y_c + y_p$.

Initial-value problem

$$ay'' + by' + cy = f(x) \text{ subject to } y(x) = y_0, \;\; y'(x_0) = y_0'$$

Find the *general solution* containing two arbitrary constants and then use the initial conditions to determine the values of the constants.

5.3 Higher order equations

The general linear equation with constant coefficents

$$a_n y^{(n)} + a_{n-1} y^{(n-1)} + \ldots + a_2 y'' + a_1 y' + a_0 y = f(x)$$

The complementary function, y_c, is found in a similar manner to that on page 33 using the auxiliary equation

$$a_n \lambda^n + a_{n-1} \lambda^{n-1} + \ldots + a_1 \lambda + a_0 = 0$$

A particular integral, y_p , is also found in a similar manner to that on page 33 using suitable trial functions.
The general solution is $y = y_c + y_p$.

Chapter 6

Fourier Series

Full-range series

$f(x)$ is defined for $-l < x < l$.

The Fourier series for $f(x)$ is given by:

$$F(x) = \frac{1}{2}a_0 + \sum_{n=1}^{\infty} a_n \cos \frac{n\pi x}{l} + \sum_{n=1}^{\infty} b_n \sin \frac{n\pi x}{l}$$

where

$$a_0 = \frac{1}{l} \int_{-l}^{l} f(x)dx,$$

$$a_n = \frac{1}{l} \int_{-l}^{l} f(x) \cos \frac{n\pi x}{l} dx; \qquad b_n = \frac{1}{l} \int_{-l}^{l} f(x) \sin \frac{n\pi x}{l} dx$$

$F(x)$ extends $f(x)$ periodically with period $2l$.

$F(x) = f(x)$ at all points, $-l < x < l$, at which f is continuous. If f is discontinuous at x_0, then $F(x_0) = \{f(x_0+) + f(x_0-)\}/2$.

Half-range series

$f(x)$ is defined for $0 < x < l$.

The Fourier half-range cosine series is:

$$F_c(x) = \frac{1}{2}a_0 + \sum_{n=1}^{\infty} a_n \cos \frac{n\pi x}{l}; \qquad a_n = \frac{2}{l} \int_{0}^{l} f(x) \cos \frac{n\pi x}{l} dx.$$

$F_c(x)$ extends $f(x)$ periodically as an even function with period $2l$.

The Fourier half-range sine series is

$$F_s(x) = \sum_{n=1}^{\infty} b_n \sin \frac{n\pi x}{l}; \qquad b_n = \frac{2}{l} \int_{0}^{l} f(x) \sin \frac{n\pi x}{l} dx.$$

$F_s(x)$ extends $f(x)$ periodically as an odd function with period $2l$.

The Fourier series of some frequently occurring functions are given on page 47.

Complex Fourier series $f(x)$ is defined for $-l < x < l$.
The complex Fourier series for $f(x)$ is given by

$$F(x) = \sum_{n=-\infty}^{\infty} c_n e^{jn\pi x/l}$$

where

$$c_n = \frac{1}{2l} \int_{-l}^{l} f(x) e^{-jn\pi x/l} dx = \begin{cases} (a_n - jb_n)/2 & n > 0 \\ a_0/2 & n = 0 \\ (a_{-n} + jb_{-n})/2 & n < 0 \end{cases}$$

The constant term, *i.e.* $\frac{1}{2}a_0$ or c_0, is the average value of $f(x)$ over the interval $(-l, l)$.

Parseval's theorem

$$\frac{1}{2l} \int_{-l}^{l} [f(x)]^2 dx = \frac{1}{4}a_0^2 + \sum_{n=1}^{\infty} \frac{1}{2}(a_n^2 + b_n^2) = \sum_{n=-\infty}^{\infty} |c_n|^2$$

Chapter 7

Vector Calculus

7.1   grad, div and curl

$$\text{Nabla operator } \nabla = \hat{\mathbf{i}}\frac{\partial}{\partial x} + \hat{\mathbf{j}}\frac{\partial}{\partial y} + \hat{\mathbf{k}}\frac{\partial}{\partial z}$$

$$\text{grad}\phi \equiv \nabla\phi = \frac{\partial\phi}{\partial x}\hat{\mathbf{i}} + \frac{\partial\phi}{\partial y}\hat{\mathbf{j}} + \frac{\partial\phi}{\partial z}\hat{\mathbf{k}}$$

$$\text{div}\mathbf{F} \equiv \nabla.\mathbf{F} = \frac{\partial F_1}{\partial x} + \frac{\partial F_2}{\partial y} + \frac{\partial F_3}{\partial z}$$

$$\text{curl}\mathbf{F} \equiv \nabla \times \mathbf{F} = \begin{vmatrix} \hat{\mathbf{i}} & \hat{\mathbf{j}} & \hat{\mathbf{k}} \\ \partial/\partial x & \partial/\partial y & \partial/\partial z \\ F_1 & F_2 & F_3 \end{vmatrix}$$

$$= (\frac{\partial F_3}{\partial y} - \frac{\partial F_2}{\partial z})\hat{\mathbf{i}} + (\frac{\partial F_1}{\partial z} - \frac{\partial F_3}{\partial x})\hat{\mathbf{j}} + (\frac{\partial F_2}{\partial x} - \frac{\partial F_1}{\partial y})\hat{\mathbf{k}}$$

$$\text{grad } \phi = \frac{\partial\phi}{\partial n}\hat{\mathbf{n}}$$

where $\hat{\mathbf{n}}$ is the unit vector normal to the surface $\phi = $ constant.

Directional derivative. The rate of change of a scalar field, ϕ, in the direction of the unit vector $\hat{\mathbf{n}}$ is given by

$$\frac{\partial\phi}{\partial n} = \text{grad } \phi.\hat{\mathbf{n}}$$

If δV is volume bounded by the surface δS then

$$\text{grad}\phi = \lim_{\delta V \to 0} \frac{1}{\delta V} \int_{\delta S} \phi d\mathbf{S}$$

$$\text{div}\mathbf{A} = \lim_{\delta V \to 0} \frac{1}{\delta V} \int_{\delta S} \mathbf{A}.d\mathbf{S}$$

$$\text{curl}\mathbf{A} = \lim_{\delta V \to 0} \frac{1}{\delta V} \int_{\delta S} d\mathbf{S} \times \mathbf{A}$$

Laplacian operator

$$\nabla^2 \equiv \nabla.\nabla = \frac{\partial^2}{\partial x^2} + \frac{\partial^2}{\partial y^2} + \frac{\partial^2}{\partial z^2}$$

Vector identities

$$\nabla(\phi\psi) = \phi\nabla\psi + \psi\nabla\phi \qquad\qquad \nabla(\phi + \psi) = \nabla\phi + \nabla\psi$$

$$\nabla.(\phi\mathbf{A}) = \mathbf{A}.\nabla\phi + \phi\nabla.\mathbf{A} \qquad\qquad \nabla.(\mathbf{A}+\mathbf{B}) = \nabla.\mathbf{A} + \nabla.\mathbf{B}$$

$$\nabla \times (\phi\mathbf{A}) = \nabla\phi \times \mathbf{A} + \phi\nabla \times \mathbf{A} \qquad \nabla \times (\mathbf{A}+\mathbf{B}) = \nabla \times \mathbf{A} + \nabla \times \mathbf{B}$$
$$\nabla.(\mathbf{A} \times \mathbf{B}) = (\nabla \times \mathbf{A}).\mathbf{B} - \mathbf{A}.(\nabla \times \mathbf{B})$$

$$\nabla \times (\nabla\phi) = \mathbf{0} \qquad\qquad \nabla.(\nabla \times \mathbf{A}) = 0$$
$$\nabla \times (\nabla \times \mathbf{A}) = \nabla(\nabla.\mathbf{A}) - \nabla^2\mathbf{A}$$

$$\nabla^2(\phi + \psi) = \nabla^2\phi + \nabla^2\psi \qquad\qquad \nabla^2(\phi\psi) = \phi\nabla^2\psi + 2\nabla\phi.\nabla\psi + \psi\nabla^2\phi$$

$$\nabla(\mathbf{A}.\mathbf{B}) = (\mathbf{A}.\nabla)\mathbf{B} + (\mathbf{B}.\nabla)\mathbf{A} + \mathbf{A} \times (\nabla \times \mathbf{B}) + \mathbf{B} \times (\nabla \times \mathbf{A})$$
$$\nabla \times (\mathbf{A} \times \mathbf{B}) = \mathbf{A}(\nabla.\mathbf{B}) - \mathbf{B}(\nabla.\mathbf{A}) + (\mathbf{B}.\nabla)\mathbf{A} - (\mathbf{A}.\nabla)\mathbf{B}$$

Cylindrical polar coordinates

$$\nabla\psi = \frac{\partial\psi}{\partial R}\hat{\mathbf{R}} + \frac{1}{R}\frac{\partial\psi}{\partial\phi}\hat{\boldsymbol{\phi}} + \frac{\partial\psi}{\partial z}\hat{\mathbf{k}}$$
$$\nabla^2\psi = \frac{1}{R}\frac{\partial}{\partial R}(R\frac{\partial\psi}{\partial R}) + \frac{1}{R^2}\frac{\partial^2\psi}{\partial\phi^2} + \frac{\partial^2\psi}{\partial z^2}$$

$$\nabla.\mathbf{A} = \frac{1}{R}\frac{\partial}{\partial R}(RA_R) + \frac{1}{R}\frac{\partial A_\phi}{\partial\phi} + \frac{\partial A_z}{\partial z}$$

$$\nabla \times \mathbf{A} = \left\{\frac{1}{R}\frac{\partial A_z}{\partial\phi} - \frac{\partial A_\phi}{\partial z}\right\}\hat{\mathbf{R}} + \left\{\frac{\partial A_R}{\partial z} - \frac{\partial A_z}{\partial R}\right\}\hat{\boldsymbol{\phi}} + \frac{1}{R}\left\{\frac{\partial}{\partial R}(RA_\phi) - \frac{\partial A_R}{\partial\phi}\right\}\hat{\mathbf{k}}$$

Spherical polar coordinates

$$\nabla\psi = \frac{\partial\psi}{\partial r}\hat{\mathbf{r}} + \frac{1}{r}\frac{\partial\psi}{\partial\theta}\hat{\boldsymbol{\theta}} + \frac{1}{r\sin\theta}\frac{\partial\psi}{\partial\phi}\hat{\boldsymbol{\phi}}$$

$$\nabla^2\psi = \frac{1}{r^2}\frac{\partial}{\partial r}\left(r^2\frac{\partial\psi}{\partial r}\right) + \frac{1}{r^2\sin\theta}\frac{\partial}{\partial\theta}\left(\sin\theta\frac{\partial\psi}{\partial\theta}\right) + \frac{1}{r^2\sin^2\theta}\frac{\partial^2\psi}{\partial\phi^2}$$

$$\nabla\cdot\mathbf{A} = \frac{1}{r^2}\frac{\partial}{\partial r}(r^2 A_r) + \frac{1}{r\sin\theta}\frac{\partial}{\partial\theta}(\sin\theta A_\theta) + \frac{1}{r\sin\theta}\frac{\partial A_\phi}{\partial\phi}$$

$$\nabla\times\mathbf{A} = \frac{1}{r\sin\theta}\left\{\frac{\partial}{\partial\theta}(\sin\theta A_\phi) - \frac{\partial A_\theta}{\partial\phi}\right\}\hat{\mathbf{r}} + \frac{1}{r\sin\theta}\left\{\frac{\partial A_r}{\partial\theta} - \sin\theta\frac{\partial}{\partial r}(rA_\phi)\right\}\hat{\boldsymbol{\theta}}$$

$$+\frac{1}{r}\left\{\frac{\partial}{\partial r}(rA_\theta) - \frac{\partial A_r}{\partial\theta}\right\}\hat{\boldsymbol{\phi}}$$

General orthogonal curvilinear coordinates

Transformation from $\mathbf{x} = (x_1, x_2, x_3,)$ to $\mathbf{u} = (u_1, u_2, u_3)$

where $\quad x_i = x_i(u_1, u_2, u_3) \quad i = 1, 2, 3$

$\qquad d\mathbf{x} = (du_1 h_1\hat{\mathbf{e}}_1, du_2 h_2\hat{\mathbf{e}}, du_3 h_3\hat{\mathbf{e}}_3)$

where $\quad h_i$ are scale factors (metric coefficients)

$\qquad \hat{\mathbf{e}}_i$ are unit vectors

and $\qquad h_i\hat{\mathbf{e}}_i = \dfrac{\partial\mathbf{x}}{\partial u_i} \quad h_i = \left|\dfrac{\partial\mathbf{x}}{\partial u_i}\right| \quad i = 1, 2, 3$

Element of arc $dl = \left[h_1^2(du_1)^2 + h_2^2(du_2)^2 + h_3^2(du_3)^2\right]^{1/2}$

Area element on u_1-coordinate surface $dA = h_2 h_3 du_2 du_3$

Volume element $dV = h_1 h_2 h_3 du_1 du_2 du_3$

Vector calculus

$$\mathrm{grad}\psi = \nabla\psi = \frac{1}{h_1}\frac{\partial\psi}{\partial u_1}\hat{\mathbf{e}}_1 + \frac{1}{h_2}\frac{\partial\psi}{\partial u_2}\hat{\mathbf{e}}_2 + \frac{1}{h_3}\frac{\partial\psi}{\partial u_3}\hat{\mathbf{e}}_3$$

$$\mathbf{A} = \mathbf{A}_1\hat{\mathbf{e}}_1 + \mathbf{A}_2\hat{\mathbf{e}}_2 + \mathbf{A}_3\hat{\mathbf{e}}_3$$

$$\mathrm{div}\mathbf{A} = \nabla\cdot\mathbf{A} = \frac{1}{h_1 h_2 h_3}\left[\frac{\partial}{\partial u_1}(A_1 h_2 h_3)\frac{\partial}{\partial u_2}(A_2 h_3 h_1)\frac{\partial}{\partial u_3}(A_3 h_1 h_2)\right]$$

$$\mathrm{curl}\mathbf{A} = \nabla\times\mathbf{A} = \frac{1}{h_1 h_2 h_3}\begin{vmatrix} h_1\hat{\mathbf{e}}_1 & h_2\hat{\mathbf{e}}_2 & h_3\hat{\mathbf{e}}_3 \\ \dfrac{\partial}{\partial u_1} & \dfrac{\partial}{\partial u_2} & \dfrac{\partial}{\partial u_3} \\ h_1 A_1 & h_2 A_2 & h_3 A_3 \end{vmatrix}$$

$$\nabla^2\psi = \frac{1}{h_1 h_2 h_3}\left[\frac{\partial}{\partial u_1}\left[\frac{h_2 h_3}{h_1}\frac{\partial\psi}{\partial u_1}\right] + \frac{\partial}{\partial u_2}\left[\frac{h_3 h_1}{h_2}\frac{\partial\psi}{\partial u_2}\right] + \frac{\partial}{\partial u_3}\left[\frac{h_1 h_2}{h_3}\frac{\partial\psi}{\partial u_3}\right]\right]$$

7.2   Integral theorems of the vector calculus

V is the volume bounded by the closed surface S

Gauss's divergence theorem

$$\int_V \mathrm{div}\mathbf{F}\,dV = \int_S \mathbf{F}.d\mathbf{S}$$

Green's theorem

First form:

$$\int_V (\phi\nabla^2\psi + \mathrm{grad}\phi.\mathrm{grad}\psi)dV = \int_S \phi\,\mathrm{grad}\psi.d\mathbf{S}$$

Second form:

$$\int_V (\phi\nabla^2\psi - \psi\nabla^2\phi)dV = \int_S (\phi\frac{\partial\psi}{\partial n} - \psi\frac{\partial\phi}{\partial n})d\mathbf{S}$$

C is the curve bounding the open surface S

Stokes's theorem

$$\int_S \mathrm{curl}\mathbf{F}.d\mathbf{S} = \int_C \mathbf{F}.d\mathbf{s} = \int_C \mathbf{F}.d\mathbf{r}$$

Chapter 8

Tables of Transforms

8.1 The Laplace transform

$$\mathcal{L}[f(t)] = \int_0^\infty e^{-st}f(t)dt \quad \text{or} \quad \mathcal{L}[x(t)] = \int_0^\infty e^{-st}x(t)dt$$
$$= F(s) \qquad\qquad\qquad\qquad = \bar{x}(s)$$

$$f(t) = \mathcal{L}^{-1}[F(s)] \qquad\qquad x(t) = \mathcal{L}^{-1}[\bar{x}(s)]$$

Table of Laplace transforms 1

$f(t)$ $\mathcal{L}^{-1}[F(s)]$	$\mathcal{L}[f(t)]$ $F(s)$	
1	$\dfrac{1}{s}$	(8.1)
t	$\dfrac{1}{s^2}$	(8.2)
t^n	$\dfrac{n!}{s^{n+1}}$	(8.3)
(n a positive integer)		
$t^\lambda (\lambda > 1)$	$\dfrac{\Gamma(\lambda+1)}{s^{\lambda+1}}$	(8.4)
e^{-at}	$\dfrac{1}{s+a}$	(8.5)
$\sin bt$	$\dfrac{b}{s^2+b^2}$	(8.6)
$\cos bt$	$\dfrac{s}{s^2+b^2}$	(8.7)
$\sin(at+\phi)$	$\dfrac{s\sin\phi + a\cos\phi}{s^2+a^2}$	(8.8)

continued...

Table of Laplace transforms 2

$f(t)$ $\mathcal{L}^{-1}[F(s)]$	$\mathcal{L}[f(t)]$ $F(s)$	
$\sinh bt$	$\dfrac{b}{s^2 - b^2}$	(8.9)
$\cosh bt$	$\dfrac{s}{s^2 - b^2}$	(8.10)
$t \sin bt$	$\dfrac{2bs}{(s^2 + b^2)^2}$	(8.11)
$t \cos bt$	$\dfrac{s^2 - b^2}{(s^2 + b^2)^2}$	(8.12)
$\sin bt - bt \cos bt$	$\dfrac{2b^3}{(s^2 + b^2)^2}$	(8.13)
$\sin bt + bt \cos bt$	$\dfrac{2bs^2}{(s^2 + b^2)^2}$	(8.14)
$e^{-at}t^n$ (n a positive integer)	$\dfrac{n!}{(s + a)^{n+1}}$	(8.15)
$e^{-at} \sin bt$	$\dfrac{b}{(s + a)^2 + b^2}$	(8.16)
$e^{-at} \cos bt$	$\dfrac{s + a}{(s + a)^2 + b^2}$	(8.17)
$e^{-at} \sinh bt$	$\dfrac{b}{(s + a)^2 - b^2}$	(8.18)
$e^{-at} \cosh bt$	$\dfrac{s + a}{(s + a)^2 - b^2}$	(8.19)
$H(t)$	$\dfrac{1}{s}$	(8.20)
$H(t - a)$	$\dfrac{e^{-as}}{s}$	(8.21)
$H(t) - H(t - a)$	$\dfrac{1 - e^{-as}}{s}$	(8.22)
$\delta(t)$	1	(8.23)
$\delta(t - a)$	e^{-as}	(8.24)
$[t]$	$\dfrac{e^{-as}}{s(1 - e^{-s})}$	(8.25)
$\dfrac{\sin at}{t}$	$\tan^{-1} \dfrac{a}{s}$	(8.26)

continued. . .

Table of Laplace transforms 3

$f(t)$ $\mathcal{L}^{-1}[F(s)]$	$\mathcal{L}[f(t)]$ $F(s)$	
$\dfrac{\cos 2\sqrt{at}}{\sqrt{\pi t}}$	$\dfrac{e^{-a/s}}{\sqrt{s}}$	(8.27)
$\operatorname{erfc}\left(\dfrac{a}{2\sqrt{t}}\right)$	$\dfrac{e^{-a\sqrt{s}}}{s}$	(8.28)
$\dfrac{a}{2\sqrt{\pi t^3}}e^{-a^2/4t}$	$e^{-a\sqrt{s}}$	(8.29)
$\dfrac{e^{-a^2/4t}}{\sqrt{\pi t}}$	$\dfrac{e^{-a\sqrt{s}}}{\sqrt{s}}$	(8.30)
$2\sqrt{\dfrac{t}{\pi}}e^{-a^2/4t} - a\operatorname{erfc}\left(\dfrac{a}{2\sqrt{t}}\right)$	$\dfrac{e^{-a\sqrt{s}}}{\sqrt{s^3}}$	(8.31)
$\dfrac{2a}{\sqrt{\pi}}e^{-a^2t^2}$	$\operatorname{erfc}\left(\dfrac{s}{2a}\right)e^{s^2/4a^2}$	(8.32)
$\alpha f(t) + \beta g(t)$	$\alpha F(s) + \beta G(s)$	(8.33)
$H(t-a)f(t-a)$	$e^{-as}F(s)$	(8.34)
$e^{-at}f(t)$	$F(s+a)$	(8.35)
$f'(t)$	$sF(s) - f(0)$	(8.36)
$f''(t)$	$s^2F(s) - sf(0) - f'(0)$	(8.37)
$f^{(n)}(t)$	$s^nF(s) - s^{n-1}f(0) - s^{n-2}f'(0) -$	
	$\ldots - f^{n-1}(0)$	(8.38)
$\displaystyle\int_0^t f(u)du$	$\dfrac{F(s)}{s}$	(8.39)
$-tf(t)$	$F'(s)$	(8.40)
$(-t)^n f(t)$	$F^{(n)}(s)$	(8.41)
$\dfrac{f(t)}{t}$	$\displaystyle\int_s^\infty F(u)du$	(8.42)
$\displaystyle\int_0^t f(u)g(t-u)du$ (convolution integral)	$F(s)G(s)$	(8.43)
$f(t+T) = f(t)$	$\dfrac{1}{1-e^{-Ts}}\displaystyle\int_0^T e^{-su}f(u)du$	(8.44)
$\displaystyle\sum_{k=1}^n \dfrac{P(\alpha_k)}{Q'(\alpha_k)}\exp(\alpha_k t)$	$P(s)/Q(s)$	(8.45)
P polynomial of degree less than n	$Q(s) = (s-\alpha_1)(s-\alpha_2)\ldots(s-\alpha_n)$ where $\alpha_1, \alpha_2, \ldots, \alpha_n$ are all distinct	

Limiting theorems $\qquad \lim_{s \to \infty} F(s) = 0, \qquad \lim_{t \to \infty} f(t) = \lim_{s \to 0} sF(s)$

Inversion formula

$$\frac{1}{2\pi j} \int_{\gamma-j\infty}^{\gamma+j\infty} e^{st} F(s) ds = \left\{ \begin{array}{ll} f(t) & t > 0 \\ 0 & t < 0 \end{array} \right.$$

Stehfest numerical inversion

Given $\bar{f}(s)$, the Laplace transform of $f(t)$, seek the value $f(T)$ for a specific value $t = T$.

Choose $s_j = j\dfrac{\ln 2}{T} \quad j = 1, 2, \ldots, M$ where M is even.

The approximate numerical inversion is given by

$$f(T) \approx \frac{\ln 2}{T} \sum_{j=1}^{M} w_j \bar{f}(s_j)$$

where the weights, w_j, are given by

$$w_j = (-1)^{\frac{M}{2}+j} \sum_{k=\left[\frac{1}{2}(1+j)\right]}^{\min(j,\frac{M}{2})} \frac{k^{\frac{M}{2}}(2k)!}{(\frac{M}{2}-k)!k!(k-1)!(j-k)!(2k-j)!}$$

Stehfest's weights for $M = 6, 8, 10, 12$ and 14

$M = 6$	$M = 8$	$M = 10$	$M = 12$	$M = 14$
1	-1/3	1/12	-1/60	1/360
-49	145/3	-385/12	961/60	-461/72
366	-906	1279	-1247	18481/20
-858	16394/3	-46871/3	82663/3	-6227627/180
810	-43130/3	505465/6	-1579685/6	4862890/9
-270	18730	-473915/2	13241387/10	-131950391/30
	-35840/3	1127735/3	-58375583/15	189788326/9
	8960/3	-1020215/3	21159859/3	-2877521087/45
		328125/2	-16010673/2	2551951591/20
		-65625/2	11105661/2	-2041646257/12
			-10777536/5	4509824011/30
			1796256/5	-169184323/2
				824366543/30
				-117766649/30

8.2 The Z-transform

$$Z\left[x(n)\right] = \sum_{n=0}^{\infty} x(n)z^{-n} = \bar{x}(z), \qquad x(n) = Z^{-1}\left[\bar{x}(z)\right]$$

Table of Z-transforms
The variable t is related to the sampling interval, T, by $t = nT$.

$x(n)$ $Z^{-1}\left[\bar{x}(z)\right]$	$Z\left[x(n)\right]$ $\bar{x}(z)$	
$\delta(n)$	1	(8.46)
1 or $H(n)$	$\dfrac{z}{z-1}$	(8.47)
n	$\dfrac{Tz}{(z-1)^2}$	(8.48)
n^2	$\dfrac{T^2 z(z+1)}{(z-1)^3}$	(8.49)
$\begin{pmatrix} n \\ k \end{pmatrix}$	$\dfrac{z}{(z-1)^{k+1}}$	(8.50)
a^n	$\dfrac{z}{z-a}$	(8.51)
$\delta(n-m)$	z^{-m}	(8.52)
e^{-an}	$\dfrac{z}{z-e^{-aT}}$	(8.53)
$\sin(an)$	$\dfrac{z\sin(aT)}{z^2 - 2z\cos(aT) + 1}$	(8.54)
ne^{-an}	$\dfrac{Tze^{-aT}}{(z-e^{-aT})^2}$	(8.55)
$\cos(an)$	$\dfrac{z^2 - z\cos(aT)}{z^2 - 2z\cos(aT) + 1}$	(8.56)
$\alpha x_1(n) + \beta x_2(n)$	$\alpha \bar{x}_1(z) + \beta \bar{x}_2(z)$	(8.57)
$x(n-m)$	$z^{-m}\bar{x}(z)$	(8.58)
$e^{-an}x(n)$	$\bar{x}(ze^{aT})$	(8.59)
$a^{-n}x(n)$	$\bar{x}(az)$	(8.60)
$x(n+1)$	$z\left[\bar{x}(z) - x(0)\right]$	(8.61)
$x(n+2)$	$z^2\left[\bar{x}(z) - x(1)z^{-1} - x(0)\right]$	(8.62)
$\displaystyle\sum_{m=0}^{n} x(m)y(n-m)$	$\bar{x}(z)\bar{y}(z)$	(8.63)

Limiting theorems

$$\lim_{n\to\infty} x(n) = \lim_{z\to 1} \frac{z-1}{z}\bar{x}(z), \quad \lim_{n\to 0} x(n) = \lim_{z\to\infty} \bar{x}(z)$$

45

8.3   The Fourier transform

$$\mathcal{F}\left[f(x)\right] = \frac{1}{\sqrt{2\pi}}\int_{-\infty}^{\infty} f(x)e^{-j\xi x}dx \qquad \mathcal{F}^{-1}\left[F(\xi)\right] = \frac{1}{\sqrt{2\pi}}\int_{-\infty}^{\infty} F(\xi)e^{j\xi x}d\xi$$
$$= F(\xi) \qquad\qquad\qquad\qquad\qquad = f(x)$$

Table of Fourier transforms

$f(x)$ $\mathcal{F}^{-1}\left[F(\xi)\right]$	$\mathcal{F}\left[f(x)\right]$ $F(\xi)$
$\dfrac{1}{\lvert x\rvert}$	$\dfrac{1}{\lvert \xi\rvert}$
$\dfrac{1}{a-jx}$	$\sqrt{2\pi}e^{-a\xi}H(\xi)$
$H(\lvert x\rvert) - H(\lvert x\rvert - a)$	$\sqrt{\dfrac{2}{\pi}}\dfrac{\sin a\xi}{\xi}$
$e^{-x^2/a}$	$\sqrt{\dfrac{a}{2}}e^{-a\xi^2/4}$
$f'(x)$	$j\xi F(\xi)$
$f''(x))$	$-\xi^2 F(\xi)$

8.4   Fourier sine and cosine transforms

$$\mathcal{F}_s\left[f(x)\right] = \sqrt{\frac{2}{\pi}}\int_0^{\infty} f(x)\sin\xi x\,dx \qquad \mathcal{F}_c\left[f(x)\right] = \sqrt{\frac{2}{\pi}}\int_o^{\infty} f(x)\cos\xi x\,dx$$
$$= F_s(\xi) \qquad\qquad\qquad\qquad\qquad = F_c(\xi)$$

$$\mathcal{F}_s^{-1}\left[F_s(\xi)\right] = \sqrt{\frac{2}{\pi}}\int_0^{\infty} F_s(\xi)\sin\xi x\,d\xi \qquad \mathcal{F}_c^{-1}\left[F_c(\xi)\right] = \sqrt{\frac{2}{\pi}}\int_0^{\infty} F_c(\xi)\cos\xi x\,d\xi$$
$$= f(x) \qquad\qquad\qquad\qquad\qquad = f(x)$$

Table of Fourier sine and cosine transforms

$f(x)$	$\mathcal{F}_s(\xi)$	$f(x)$	$\mathcal{F}_c(\xi)$
e^{-x}	$\sqrt{\dfrac{2}{\pi}}\dfrac{1}{(1+\xi^2)}$	e^{-x}	$\sqrt{\dfrac{2}{\pi}}\dfrac{1}{(1+\xi^2)}$
$xe^{-x^2/2}$	$e^{-\xi^2/2}$	e^{-x^2}	$e^{-\xi^2}$
$\dfrac{\sin x}{x}$	$\dfrac{1}{\sqrt{2\pi}}\ln\left|\dfrac{1+\xi}{1-\xi}\right|$	$H(x)-H(x-a)$	$\sqrt{\dfrac{2}{\pi}}\dfrac{\sin a\xi}{\xi}$
$f'(x)$	$-\xi\mathcal{F}_c(\xi)$	$f'(x)$	$\xi\mathcal{F}_s(\xi)-\sqrt{\dfrac{2}{\pi}}f(0)$
$f''(x)$	$-\xi^2\mathcal{F}_s(\xi)+\xi\sqrt{\dfrac{2}{\pi}}f(0)$	$f''(x)$	$-\xi^2\mathcal{F}_c(\xi)-\sqrt{\dfrac{2}{\pi}}f'(0)$

8.5 Some periodic functions: Laplace transforms and Fourier series

Graphs of the Laplace transform, $F(s)$, and the Fourier series, $F_s(x), F_c(x)$ or $F(x)$:

For the Laplace transform it is assumed that $f(x) \equiv 0$ for $x < 0$.

1. **Square wave (odd function) height h, period $2a$**

$$f(x) = \begin{cases} -h & -a \leq x < 0 \\ h & 0 \leq x < a \end{cases}$$

$$F(s) = \frac{h}{s}\tanh\left(\frac{as}{2}\right) \qquad F_s(x) = \frac{4h}{\pi}\sum_{n=0}^{\infty}\frac{1}{(2n+1)}\sin\left[\frac{(2n+1)\pi x}{a}\right]$$

2. Square wave (even function), period $2a$

$$f(x) = \begin{cases} -h & -a \le x < -a/2 \\ h & -a/2 \le x < a/2 \\ -h & a/2 \le x < a \end{cases}$$

$$F(s) = \frac{h}{s}e^{as/2}\tanh\left(\frac{as}{2}\right) \qquad F_c(x) = \frac{4h}{\pi}\sum_{n=0}^{\infty}\frac{(-1)^n}{(2n+1)}\cos\left[\frac{(2n+1)\pi x}{a}\right]$$

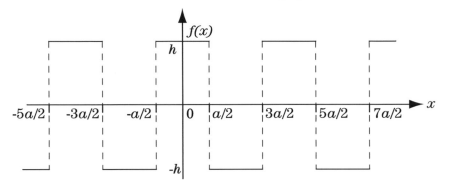

3. Triangular wave, period $2a$

$$f(x) = \begin{cases} -hx/a & -a \le x < 0 \\ hx/a & 0 \le x < a \end{cases}$$

$$F(s) = \frac{h}{as^2}\tanh\left(\frac{as}{2}\right) \qquad F_c(x) = \frac{h}{2} - \frac{4h}{\pi^2}\sum_{n=0}^{\infty}\frac{1}{(2n+1)^2}\cos\left[\frac{(2n+1)\pi x}{a}\right]$$

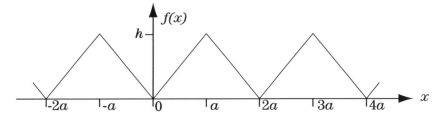

4. Sawtooth wave, period $2a$

$$f(x) = hx/2a \quad 0 \le x < 2a$$

$$F(s) = \frac{h}{2as^2} - \frac{he^{-2as}}{s(1-e^{-2as})} \qquad F(x) = \frac{h}{2} - \frac{4h}{\pi}\sum_{n=1}^{\infty}\frac{(-1)^n}{n}\sin\left[\frac{n\pi x}{2a}\right]$$

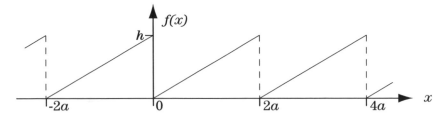

48

5. Rectified sine wave, period a

$$f(x) = h\sin(x/a) \quad 0 \le x < a$$

$$F(s) = \frac{\pi a h}{a^2 s^2 + \pi^2} \coth\left(\frac{as}{2}\right) \qquad F_c(x) = \frac{2h}{\pi} - \frac{4h}{\pi} \sum_{n=1}^{\infty} \frac{\cos(2n\pi x/a)}{(4n^2 - 1)}$$

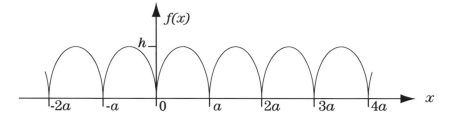

6. Half-rectified sine wave, period a

$$f(x) = \begin{cases} h\sin(2x/a) & 0 \le x < a/2 \\ 0 & a/2 \le x < a \end{cases}$$

$$F(s) = \frac{\pi a h}{(a^2 s^2 + \pi^2)(1 - e^{-as})} \qquad F(x) = \frac{h}{\pi} - \frac{2h}{\pi} \sum_{n=1}^{\infty} \frac{\cos(2n\pi x/a)}{(4n^2 - 1)} + \frac{h}{2}\sin\left(\frac{\pi x}{a}\right)$$

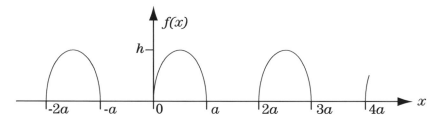

49

Chapter 9

Numerical Methods

9.1   Interpolation

Polynomial interpolation: Suppose that f is defined on the interval $-1 \leq x \leq 1$ with $n+1$ continuous derivatives. If the n-degree polynomial approximation at the $n+1$ points $x_0, x_1, \ldots, x_n$ is given by $p_n(x)$ then the error at any point $x \in (-1, 1)$ is given by

$$f(x) - p_n(x) = \frac{(x - x_0)(x - x_1) \ldots (x - x_n)}{(n+1)!} f^{(n+1)}(\xi) \text{ for some } \xi \in (-1, 1)$$

Lagrange interpolation polynomials

$$L_i(x) = \frac{(x - x_0)(x - x_1) \ldots (x - x_{i-1})(x - x_{i+1}) \ldots (x - x_n)}{(x_i - x_0)(x_i - x_1) \ldots (x_i - x_{i-1})(x_i - x_{i+1}) \ldots (x_i - x_n)}$$

The nth degree collocation polynomial through the points $(x_0, y_0), (x_1, y_1) \ldots (x_n, y_n)$ is given by

$$P_n(x) = \sum_{i=0}^{n} L_i(x) y_i$$

Cubic splines

The cubic spline interpolating function, $S(x)$, through the points $(x_0, y_0), (x_1, y_1) \ldots (x_n, y_n)$ has the properties $S(x_i) = y_i$ *i.e.* S is continuous at (x_i, y_i).

$S'(x)$ and $S''(x)$ are continuous.

$S(x)$ is a cubic polynomial, $S_i(x)$, in each interval $[x_i, x_{i+1}]$.

$$S_i(x) = \frac{y_{i+1}(x - x_i)}{h_i} - \frac{y_i(x - x_{i+1})}{h_i}$$
$$- \frac{M_i}{6} \left[\frac{(x - x_{i+1})^3}{h_i} - h_i(x - x_{i+1}) \right] - \frac{M_{i+1}}{6} \left[\frac{(x - x_i)^3}{h_i} - h_i(x - x_i) \right]$$

where M_i are found from

$$\begin{bmatrix} a_{00} & a_{01} & 0 & 0 & \cdots & 0 \\ h_0 & 2(h_0+h_1) & h_1 & 0 & \cdots & 0 \\ 0 & h_1 & 2(h_1+h_2) & h_2 & \cdots & 0 \\ \vdots & \vdots & & & & \vdots \\ 0 & \cdots & 0 & h_{n-2} & 2(h_{n-2}+h_{n-1}) & h_{n-1} \\ 0 & \cdots & 0 & 0 & a_{nn-1} & a_{nn} \end{bmatrix} \begin{bmatrix} M_0 \\ M_1 \\ M_2 \\ \vdots \\ M_{n-1} \\ M_n \end{bmatrix}$$

$$= 6 \begin{bmatrix} b_0 \\ \frac{y_2-y_1}{h_1} - \frac{y_1-y_0}{h_0} \\ \frac{y_3-y_2}{h_2} - \frac{y_2-y_1}{h_1} \\ \vdots \\ b_n \end{bmatrix}$$

where $h_i = x_{i+1} - x_i$.

Natural spline, $M_0 = M_n = 0$ so that

$$a_{00} = a_{nn} = 1, \quad a_{01} = a_{nn-1} = b_0 = b_n = 0$$

If the derivative of the underlying function is known at x_0 and y_0 then

$$a_{00} = 2h_0, \quad a_{01} = h_0, \quad b_0 = (y_1-y_0)/h_0 - f'(x_0)$$

$$a_{nn-1} = h_{n-1}, \quad a_{nn} = 2h_{n-1}, \quad b_n = f'(x_n) - (y_n - y_{n-1})/h_{n-1}$$

9.2 Finite difference operators

Forward $\quad \Delta y_i = y_{i+1} - y_i$ $\qquad$ Backward $\quad \nabla y_i = y_i - y_{i-1}$

Central $\quad \delta y_{i+\frac{1}{2}} = y_{i+1} - y_i$ $\qquad$ Shift $\quad E y_i = y_{i+1}$

Average $\quad \mu y_{i+\frac{1}{2}} = (y_i + y_{i+1})/2$ $\quad$ Differential $\quad D y_i = (dy/dx)_{x_i}$

Relationship between the operators

	E	Δ	δ, μ	∇	hD
E	E	$1+\Delta$	$1 + \mu\delta + \delta^2/2$	$(1-\nabla)^{-1}$	e^{hD}
Δ	$E-1$	Δ	$\mu\delta + \delta^2/2$	$\nabla(1-\nabla)^{-1}$	$e^{hD}-1$
δ	$E^{\frac{1}{2}} - E^{-\frac{1}{2}}$	$\Delta(1+\Delta)^{\frac{1}{2}}$	δ	$\nabla(1-\nabla)^{-\frac{1}{2}}$	$2\sinh(hD/2)$
∇	$1 - E^{-1}$	$\Delta(1+\Delta)^{-1}$	$\mu\delta - \delta^2/2$	∇	$1 - e^{-hD}$
hD	$\ln E$	$\ln(1+\Delta)$	$2\sinh^{-1}(\delta/2)$	$-\ln(1-\nabla)$	hD
μ	$(E^{\frac{1}{2}} + E^{-\frac{1}{2}})/2$		$(1+\delta^2/4)^{\frac{1}{2}}$		$\cosh(hD/2)$

9.3 Non-linear algebraic equations

Formula iteration method for $x = F(x)$.
An iterative scheme has the form $x_{n+1} = F(x_n)$, which converges to the root $x = \alpha$, only if $|F'(\alpha)| < 1$. The convergence is first order; *i.e.* if $|F'(x)| \leq M$ for x near α, then the error at each stage satisfies $|\epsilon_{n+1}| \leq M|\epsilon_n|$.

Newton-Raphson method for $f(x) = 0$.

$$x_{n+1} = x_n - \frac{f(x_n)}{f'(x_n)}$$

The method converges to the root $x = \alpha$ if x_0 is sufficiently close to α. The convergence is second order *i.e.* if $|f''(x)| \leq 2M$ for x near α then the error at each stage satisfies $|\epsilon_{n+1}| \leq M|\epsilon_n|^2$.

Newton's method for a system of equations $\mathbf{f}(\mathbf{x}) = \mathbf{0}$, where $\mathbf{f} = \{f_1(\mathbf{x}), f_2(\mathbf{x}), \ldots, f_n(\mathbf{x})\}$ and $\mathbf{x} = \{x_1, x_2, \ldots, x_n\}$.

$$\mathbf{x}^{(n+1)} = \mathbf{x}^{(n)} - \mathbf{J}_n^{-1}\mathbf{f}(\mathbf{x}^{(n)})$$

where $\mathbf{J}_n$ is the Jacobian matrix given by

$$(\mathbf{J}_n)_{ij} = \left[\frac{\partial f_i}{\partial x_j}(\mathbf{x}^{(n)})\right]$$

9.4 Numerical integration

The region of integration is subdivided into n equal intervals of width $h = (b-a)/n$, $x_i = a + ih$ and $f_i = f(x_i)$.

Trapezoidal rule

$$\int_a^b f(x)dx \approx h\left\{(f_0 + f_n)/2 + (f_1 + f_2 + \ldots + f_{n-1})\right\}$$

The error, ϵ_n, is bounded as follows:

$$|\epsilon_n| \leq (b-a)\frac{h^2}{12}M_1, \text{ where } M_1 = \max_{x \in [a,b]}|f''(x)|$$

Simpson's rule (n must be even)

$$\int_a^b f(x)dx \approx \frac{h}{3}\left\{f_0 + f_n + 4(f_1 + f_3 + \ldots + f_{n-1}) + 2(f_2 + f_4 + \ldots + f_{n-2})\right\}$$

The error, ϵ_n, is bounded as follows:

$$|\epsilon_n| \le (b-a)\frac{h^4}{180}M_2, \text{ where } M_2 = \max_{x\in[a,b]}|f^{(\text{iv})}(x)|$$

Gauss quadrature

Whenever $f(x)$ is known explicitly Gauss quadrature can be employed:

$$\int_{-1}^{1} f(x)dx \approx \sum_{i=1}^{n}\omega_i f(x_i)$$

The error, ϵ_n, is bounded as follows:

$$|\epsilon_n| \le \frac{2^{2n+1}(n!)^4}{(2n+1)[(2n)!]^3}M_3 \text{ where } M_3 = \max_{x\in[-1,1]}|f^{(2n)}(x)|$$

Gauss quadrature: integration points and weights

n	$\pm x_i$	ω_i
1	0.00000 00000 00000	2.00000 00000 00000
2	0.57735 02691 89626	1.00000 00000 00000
3	0.00000 00000 00000	0.88888 88888 88889
	0.77459 66692 41483	0.55555 55555 55556
4	0.33998 10435 84856	0.65214 51548 62546
	0.86113 63115 94053	0.34785 48451 37454
5	0.00000 00000 00000	0.56888 88888 88889
	0.53846 93101 05683	0.47862 86704 99366
	0.90617 98459 38664	0.23692 68850 56189
6	0.23861 91860 83197	0.46791 39345 72691
	0.66120 93864 66265	0.36076 15730 48139
	0.93246 95142 03152	0.17132 44923 79170

The x_i are the positive zeros of the Legendre polynomial $P_n(x)$. The formula integrates exactly all polynomials of degree $2n-1$. Any interval $a \le X \le b$ can be transformed to the interval $-1 \le x \le 1$ by the change of variable

$$X = (a+b)/2 + (b-a)x/2$$

For double integrals:

$$\int_{-1}^{1}\int_{-1}^{1} f(x,y)dxdy \approx \sum_{i=1}^{n}\sum_{j=1}^{n}\omega_i\omega_j f(x_i,y_i)$$

9.5 Numerical solution of ordinary differential equations

First order equations

$$y' = f(x, y) \text{ with } y(x_0) = y_0$$

The equation is solved successively at discrete points $x_1, x_2, x_3, \ldots$
where $x_{i+1} - x_i = h$.
y_n is the exact value $y(x_n)$.
Y_n is the approximation to y_n, used in the recurrence relation.

Single-step methods
Euler's method

$$Y_{i+1} = Y_i + h f(x_i, Y_i), \quad Y_0 = y_0$$

The error is $\dfrac{h^2}{2} y''(\xi)$ where $x_i < \xi < x_{i+1}$.

Modified Euler method

$$Y_{i+1} = Y_i + \frac{h}{2} \left\{ f(x_i, Y_i) + f(x_{i+1}, Y_{i+1}^P) \right\}, \quad Y_0 = y_0$$

where $Y_{i+1}^P = Y_i + h f(x_i, Y_i)$
The error is $-\dfrac{h^3}{12} y'''(\xi)$ where $x_i < \xi < x_{i+1}$.

Runge-Kutta (fourth order formulae)

$$Y_{i+1} = Y_i + \frac{1}{6}(k_1 + 2k_2 + 2k_3 + k_4), \quad Y_0 = y_0$$

where $\quad k_1 = h f(x_i, Y_i), \qquad\qquad k_2 = h f(x_i + h/2, Y_i + k_1/2),$
$\qquad k_3 = h f(x_i + h/2, Y_i + k_2/2), \quad k_4 = h f(x_i + h, Y_i + k_3).$
The actual form of the local truncation error, ϵ_{i+1}, is extremely complicated; it is, however, of the order h^5.

Multi-step methods (Predictor-corrector)
Milne-Simpson method
Predict $Y_{i+1}^P = Y_{i-3} + \dfrac{4h}{3}[2f_i - f_{i-1} + 2f_{i-2}]$

Correct $Y_{i+1}^C = Y_{i-1} + \dfrac{h}{3}[f_{i-1} + 4f_i + f_{i+1}^P]$

The error in the predictor is $\dfrac{14}{45} h^5 y^{(\mathrm{v})}(\xi_1)$

and the error in the corrector is $-\dfrac{h^5}{90} y^{(\mathrm{v})}(\xi_2)$
where $x_{i-3} < \xi_1 < x_{i+1}, \quad x_{i-1} < \xi_2 < x_{i+1}$.

54

Adams-Moulton method

Predict $Y_{i+1}^P = Y_i + \dfrac{h}{24}[55f_i - 59f_{i-1} + 37f_{i-2} - 9f_{i-3}]$

Correct $Y_{i+1}^C = Y_i + \dfrac{h}{24}[f_{i-2} - 5f_{i-1}^P + 19f_i + 9f_{i+1}]$

The error in the predictor is $\dfrac{14}{45}h^5 y^{(v)}(\xi_1)$

and the error in the corrector is $-\dfrac{h^5}{90}y^{(v)}(\xi_2)$

where $x_i < \xi_1 < x_{i+1}$ and $x_i < \xi_2 < x_{i+1}$.

Higher order equations

The methods given above are easily generalised for use with a system of first order equations, thus we consider only the first order equation in one dependent variable.

The nth order equation $y^{(n)} = f(x, y, y', \ldots, y^{(n-1)})$ may be reduced to the system of first order equations

$$y_1' = y, \quad y_2 = y_1', \quad y_3 = y_2', \quad \ldots \quad y_{n-1} = y_{n-2}'$$
$$y_n' = f(x, y_1, y_2, \ldots, y_n)$$
$$i.e.\ \mathbf{y}' = \mathbf{f}(x, \mathbf{y})$$

The corresponding Euler recurrence relation is

$$\mathbf{Y}_{i+1} = \mathbf{Y}_i + h\mathbf{f}(x_i, \mathbf{y}_i), \quad \mathbf{Y}_0 = \mathbf{y}_0$$

9.6 Systems of linear equations, $n \times n$

$$
\begin{array}{llll}
a_{11}x_1+ & a_{12}x_2 + \ldots + & a_{1n}x_n = & b_1 \\
a_{21}x_1+ & a_{22}x_2 + \ldots + & a_{2n}x_n = & b_2 \\
\vdots & \vdots & \vdots & \vdots \\
a_{n1}x_1+ & a_{n2}x_2 + \ldots + & a_{nn}x_n = & b_n
\end{array}
\qquad \text{in matrix form } \mathbf{Ax=b}
$$

Direct method

Gauss elimination, with partial pivoting

Computational procedure, $(k = 1 \ldots (n-1))$:

1. Rearrange the equations so that
   $|a_{kk}| \geq |a_{ik}|, \quad i = (k+1)(1)n$

2. Compute
   $\mu_{ik} = -a_{ik}/a_{kk}, \quad i = (k+1)\ldots n$

3. Compute
   $\left. \begin{array}{l} a_{ij}' = a_{ij} + \mu_{ik}a_{kj}, \quad j = (k+1)\ldots n \\ b_i' = b_i + \mu_{ik}b_k \end{array} \right\}$

4. Compute

$$x_n = b'_n / a'_{nn}$$

$$x_i = \left(b'_i - \sum_{j=i+1}^{n} a'_{ij} x_j \right) / a'_{ii}, \quad i = (n-1) \ldots 1$$

Indirect methods

Jacobi

An iterative scheme is given by

$$x_i^{(r+1)} = \frac{1}{a_{ii}} \left(b_i - \sum_{j=1}^{n}{}' a_{ij} x_j^{(r)} \right), \quad i = 1, 2, \ldots, n$$

In matrix form

$$\mathbf{x}^{(r+1)} = \mathbf{b} - [\mathbf{L} + \mathbf{U}]\mathbf{x}^{(r)}$$

Gauss-Seidel

An iterative scheme is given by

$$x_i^{(r+1)} = \frac{1}{a_{ii}} \left(b_i - \sum_{j=1}^{i-1} a_{ij} x_j^{(r+1)} - \sum_{j=i+1}^{n} a_{ij} x_j^{(r)} \right), \quad i = 1, 2, \ldots, n.$$

A sufficient condition for convergence of both methods is that the matrix $\mathbf{A}$ is *diagonally dominant*
i.e.

$$|a_{ii}| > \sum_{\substack{j=1 \\ j \neq 1}}^{n} |a_{ij}|, \quad i = 1, 2, \ldots, n$$

In matrix form

$$\mathbf{x}^{(r+1)} = \mathbf{b} - \mathbf{L}\mathbf{x}^{(r+a)} - \mathbf{U}\mathbf{X}^{(r)}$$

where

$$\mathbf{L} = \begin{bmatrix} 0 & 0 & 0 & 0 & 0 \\ \frac{a_{21}}{a_{22}} & 0 & 0 & 0 & 0 \\ \frac{a_{31}}{a_{33}} & \frac{a_{32}}{a_{33}} & 0 & 0 & 0 \\ \vdots & \vdots & & & \\ \frac{a_{n1}}{a_{nn}} & \frac{a_{n2}}{a_{nn}} & \cdots & \frac{a_{nn-1}}{a_{nn}} & 0 \end{bmatrix}, \mathbf{U} = \begin{bmatrix} 0 & \frac{a_{12}}{a_{11}} & \frac{a_{13}}{a_{11}} & \cdots & \frac{a_{1n}}{a_{11}} \\ 0 & 0 & \frac{a_{23}}{a_{22}} & \cdots & \frac{a_{2n}}{a_{22}} \\ & & & & \vdots \\ 0 & 0 & 0 & 0 & \frac{a_{n-1n}}{a_{n-1n-1}} \\ 0 & 0 & 0 & 0 & 0 \end{bmatrix}$$

and $\mathbf{b} = [b_1/a_{11} \; b_2/a_{22} \ldots b_n/a_{nn}]^T$.

The Gauss-Seidel process converges if and only if all the eigenvalues of the matrix $[\mathbf{I} + \mathbf{L}]^{-1}\mathbf{U}$ have modulus less than one.

Successive over-relaxation (SOR)
The *SOR* iterative scheme is

$$\mathbf{x}^{(r+1)} = \mathbf{x}^{(r)} + \omega(\mathbf{b} - \mathbf{L}\mathbf{x}^{(r+1)} - \mathbf{x}^{(r)} - \mathbf{U}\mathbf{x}^{(r)}),$$

where $1 < \omega < 2$ for over-relaxation, and $\omega = 1$ for Gauss-Seidel.

The *SOR* process converges if and only if all the eigenvalues of the matrix $[\mathbf{I} + \omega\mathbf{L}]^{-1}[(1 - \omega)\mathbf{I} - \omega\mathbf{U}]$ have modulus less than one.

9.7 Chebyshev polynomials

Recurrence relation
$T_{n+1}(x) = 2xT_n(x) - T_{n-1}(x); \quad T_0(x) = 1, \quad T_1(x) = x$
$T_n(x) = \cos(n\cos^{-1}x)$ (coefficient of x^n is 2^{n-1})
$T_2(x) = 2x^2 - 1, \quad T_3(x) = 4x^3 - 3x, \quad T_4(x) = 8x^4 - 8x^2 + 1,$
$T_5(x) = 16x^5 - 20x^3 + 5x$
The polynomial $(1/2^{n-1})T_n(x)$ has a smaller upper bound to its magnitude over $[-1, 1]$ than that of any other polynomial with leading term x^n.

9.8 Numerical eigenvalues and eigenvectors

The matrix eigenvalue problem is given by, see page 13,

$$\mathbf{A}\mathbf{x} = \lambda\mathbf{x}$$

Power method
(for a non-repeated dominant eigenvalue λ_1, and eigenvector $\mathbf{x}_1$).
Let $\mathbf{z}_0$ be an arbitrary vector, but not $\mathbf{x}_1, \mathbf{x}_2, \ldots, \mathbf{x}_n$, then the iterative process $\mathbf{z}_{i+1} = \frac{1}{k_i}\mathbf{A}\mathbf{z}_i$ (where k_i is the element with the largest absolute value in $\mathbf{z}_i$) converges, with $k_i \to \lambda_1$ and $\mathbf{z}_i \to \mathbf{x}_1$, provided that $\mathbf{A}$ has n linearly independent eigenvectors. The convergence will be slow if $|\lambda_2| \approx |\lambda_1|$.

Inverse iteration

(for the eigenvalue λ closest to p and eigenvector $\mathbf{x}$)

Let $\mathbf{z}_0$ be an arbitrary vector, then the iterative process

$$\mathbf{z}_{i+1} = \frac{1}{k_i}[\mathbf{A} - p\mathbf{I}]^{-1}\mathbf{z}_i$$

converges with $k_i \to \frac{1}{\lambda - p}$ and $\mathbf{z}_i \to \mathbf{x}$, where k_i is the element with the largest absolute value in $\mathbf{z}_i$.

Jacobi method

(for symmetric matrices)

Suppose that $\mathbf{A}$ is diagonalised by using a sequence of orthogonal transformations

$$\mathbf{D} = \mathbf{T}_k^t\mathbf{T}_{k-1}^t \ldots \mathbf{T}_2^t\mathbf{T}_1^t\mathbf{A}\mathbf{T}_1\mathbf{T}_2 \ldots \mathbf{T}_{k-1}\mathbf{T}_k = \mathbf{M}^t\mathbf{A}\mathbf{M}, \text{ say,}$$

then the columns of $\mathbf{M}$ are the eigenvectors and the diagonal of $\mathbf{D}$ comprises the corresponding eigenvalues.

Computational procedure:

1. Locate largest off-diagonal element a_{pq}, say.

2. Compute θ, where $\tan 2\theta = 2a_{pq}/(a_{qq} - a_{pp})$, $\quad |\theta| \leq \pi/4$.

3. Compute new elements in rows p and q
   $a'_{pp} = a_{pp} - (\tan\theta)a_{pq} \qquad a'_{qq} = a_{qq} + (\tan\theta)a_{pq}$
   $a'_{pq} = 0$
   $a'_{pj} = (\cos\theta)a_{pj} - (\sin\theta)a_{qj} \quad a'_{qj} = (\sin\theta)a_{pj} + (\cos\theta)a_{qj}$

4. If any off-diagonal element is non-zero, return to 1.

LR method

(for all the eigenvalues)

Form the sequence $\mathbf{A}_0 = \mathbf{A}$, $\quad \mathbf{A}_{r+1} = \mathbf{U}_r\mathbf{L}_r$, where $\mathbf{A}_r = \mathbf{L}_r\mathbf{U}_r$ with $\mathbf{L}_r$ lower triangular, all diagonal elements are equal to 1 and $\mathbf{U}_r$ is upper triangular.

For suitable $\mathbf{A}$ the sequence converges to an upper triangular matrix whose diagonal elements are the eigenvalues of $\mathbf{A}$, arranged in order of decreasing modulus.

If the method fails to converge try applying it again to $\mathbf{A} + p\mathbf{I}$ where p is a suitable real number. Convergence in this case will be to $\lambda_i + p$.

9.9 Least squares approximation

Given the data set $\{(x_0, y_0), (x_1, y_1), \ldots, (x_N, y_N)\}$, the least squares best fit n^{th} degree polynomial $(n < N - 1)$ is

$$y = a_0 + a_1 x + a_2 x^2 + \ldots + a_n x^n$$

where the coefficients a_i are found from the normal equations

$$\begin{bmatrix} N & \sum x_i & \sum x_i^2 & \cdots & \sum x_i^n \\ \sum x_i & \sum x_i^2 & \sum x_i^3 & \cdots & \sum x_i^{n+1} \\ & & \sum x_i^4 & \cdots & \sum x_i^{n+2} \\ & \text{symmetric} & & \vdots & \\ & & & & \sum x_i^{2n} \end{bmatrix} \begin{bmatrix} a_0 \\ a_1 \\ a_2 \\ \vdots \\ a_n \end{bmatrix} = \begin{bmatrix} \sum y_i \\ \sum x_i y_i \\ \sum x_i^2 y_i \\ \vdots \\ \sum x_i^n y_i \end{bmatrix}$$

Chapter 10

Statistics

10.1 Sample statistics

The following definitions are concerned with the data set $x_1, x_2, \ldots, x_n$. Where appropriate, the data value x_i occurs with frequency f_i.

Sample Mean
(arithmetic)
or Average
$$\bar{x} = \frac{1}{n} \sum_{i=1}^{n} x_i \quad \text{or} \quad \sum_{i=1}^{k} f_i x_i \Big/ \sum_{i=1}^{k} f_i$$

Population variance
$$\sigma^2 = \frac{1}{n} \sum_{i=1}^{n} (x_i - \bar{x})^2 = \frac{\sum x_i^2 - \dfrac{(\sum x_i)^2}{n}}{n}$$

or

$$\sigma^2 = \frac{1}{\displaystyle\sum_{i=1}^{k} f_i} \sum_{i=1}^{k} f_i (x_i - \bar{x})^2 = \frac{\sum f_i x_i^2 - \dfrac{(\sum f_i x_i)^2}{\sum f_i}}{\sum f_i}$$

Standard deviation $\quad \sigma$

Sample variance
$$s^2 = \frac{1}{n-1} \sum_{i=1}^{n} (x_i - \bar{x})^2 = \frac{\sum x_i^2 - \dfrac{(\sum x_i)^2}{n}}{(n-1)}$$

Pooled variance
$$s_p^2 = \frac{(n_1 - 1)s_1^2 + (n_2 - 1)s_2^2}{n_1 + n_2 - 2}$$

Standard error of mean $\quad \dfrac{\sigma}{\sqrt{n}}$

10.2 Regression and correlation

Pearson's Product-moment Correlation Coefficient of n sample pairs (x_i, y_i)

$$r = \frac{\sum(x_i - \bar{x})(y_i - \bar{y})}{\sqrt{[\sum(x_i - \bar{x})^2 \sum(y_i - \bar{y})^2]}}$$

$$= \frac{\sum x_i y_i - \dfrac{(\sum x_i)(\sum y_i)}{n}}{\sqrt{\left\{\left[\sum x_i^2 - \dfrac{(\sum x_i)^2}{n}\right]\left[\sum y_i^2 - \dfrac{(\sum y_i)^2}{n}\right]\right\}}}$$

Least squares estimates a and b in the fitted regression line $\hat{y} = a + bx$

$$b = \frac{\sum(x_i - \bar{x})(y_i - \bar{y})}{\sum(x_i - \bar{x})^2} = \frac{\sum x_i y_i - \dfrac{(\sum x_i)(\sum y_i)}{n}}{\sum x_i^2 - \dfrac{(\sum x_i)^2}{n}}$$

$$a = \bar{y} - b\bar{x}$$

Residual Variance in simple linear regression

$$s^2 = \frac{1}{n-2}\sum_{i=1}^{n}(y_i - a - bx_i)^2 = \frac{SSE}{n-2}$$

Spearman's rank correlation coefficient of n pairs of sample rankings (x_i, y_i)

$$r_s = 1 - \frac{6\sum d_i^2}{n(n^2 - 1)} \text{ where } d_i = x_i - y_i$$

10.3 Distributions

Discrete uniform distribution

k: the possible number of values

Probability function
$$P(x) = \frac{1}{k}$$
$$x = x_1, x_2, \ldots, x_k$$

Mean
$$\frac{k+1}{2}$$

Variance
$$\frac{k^2 - 1}{12}$$

Hypergeometric distribution

N: population size

n: sample size

k: number of items in population labelled "success"

Probability function
$$P(x) = \frac{\dbinom{k}{x}\dbinom{N-k}{n-x}}{\dbinom{N}{n}}$$

Mean	$\dfrac{nk}{N}$
Variance	$n\dfrac{k}{N}\left(1-\dfrac{k}{N}\right)\left(\dfrac{N-n}{N-1}\right)$

Binomial distribution

n: number of trials

p: probability of "success" at each trial

Probability function	$P(x) = \begin{pmatrix} n \\ x \end{pmatrix} p^x (1-p)^{n-x}$
	$x = 0, 1, \ldots, n$
Mean	np
Variance	$np(1-p)$

Negative binomial distribution

r: no. of successes required

x: no. of the trial when the rth "success" occurs

or alternatively, if c is the number of "failures" preceding the rth "success"

Probability function	$P(x) = \begin{pmatrix} x-1 \\ r-1 \end{pmatrix} p^r (1-p)^{x-r}$
	$x = r, r+1, \ldots, \infty$
Mean	$\dfrac{r}{p}$
Variance	$\dfrac{r(1-p)}{p^2}$
Probability function	$P(c) = \begin{pmatrix} c+r-1 \\ c \end{pmatrix} p^r q^c$

the general term of the binomial expansions of $p^r(1-q)^{-r}$

Mean	$\dfrac{r(1-p)}{p}$
Variance	$\dfrac{r(1-p)}{p^2}$

Geometric distribution

p: probabililty of "success" at each trial

Probability function	$P(x) = p(1-p)^{x-1}$
	$x = 1, 2, \ldots$
Mean	$\dfrac{1}{p}$
Variance	$\dfrac{1-p}{p^2}$

Poisson distribution

m: average number of random events in a given interval

Probability function $\quad P(x) = \dfrac{e^{-m}m^x}{x!}$

$\qquad\qquad\qquad\qquad x = 0, 1, \ldots$

Mean $\qquad\qquad\qquad m$

Variance $\qquad\qquad\quad m$

Continuous uniform distribution

α: minimum value

β: maximum value

Probability function $\quad f(x; \alpha, \beta) = \dfrac{1}{\beta - \alpha}$

$\qquad\qquad\qquad\qquad \alpha \le x \le \beta$

Mean $\qquad\qquad\qquad \dfrac{\beta + \alpha}{2}$

Variance $\qquad\qquad\quad \dfrac{(\beta - \alpha)^2}{12}$

Exponential distribution

m: average number of random events in a given interval

Probability function $\quad f(x; m) = me^{-mx} \quad x > 0$

Mean $\qquad\qquad\qquad \dfrac{1}{m}$

Variance $\qquad\qquad\quad \dfrac{1}{m^2}$

Normal distribution

μ: mean

σ^2: variance

Probability function $\quad f(x; \mu, \sigma^2) = \dfrac{1}{\sigma\sqrt{2\pi}}\exp\left\{-\dfrac{1}{2}\left(\dfrac{x - \mu}{b}\right)^2\right\}$

$\qquad\qquad\qquad\qquad -\infty < x < \infty$

Mean $\qquad\qquad\qquad \mu$

Variance $\qquad\qquad\quad \sigma^2$

Chapter 11

S. I. Units (Système International d'Unités)

11.1 Fundamental units

The *kilogram* (kg) is defined as the mass of the international prototype platinum-iridium cylinder kept at Sèvres.

The *second* (s) is defined as the time taken by 9 192 631 770 periods of the radiation from the transition between the two hyperfine levels of the ground state of the atom Caesium-133.

The *metre* (m) is defined as the path length of light in a vacuum during an instant of $1/(2.99792458 \times 10^8)$ seconds.

The *mole* (mol) is defined as the amount of substance of a system which contains as many elementary entities as there are atoms in 0.012 kilograms of the isotope Carbon-12.

The *ampère* (A) is defined as that constant current which, if maintained in each of two infinitely long straight parallel wires of negligible cross-section placed 1 metre apart in vacuo, would produce, between the wires, a force 2×10^{-7} newtons per metre length.

The *kelvin* (K) is defined as the fraction $1/273.16$ of the thermodynamic temperature of the triple point of water.

The *candela* (cd) is defined as the luminous intensity from a source of monochromatic radiation of frequency 540×10^{12} Hz which has a radiant intensity of $1/683$ Watts per steradian in a given direction.

11.2 S. I. Prefixes and multiplication factors

Factor	Prefix	Symbol
10^{24}	yotta	Y
10^{21}	zetta	Z
10^{18}	exa	E
10^{15}	peta	P
10^{12}	tera	T
10^{9}	giga	G
10^{6}	mega	M
10^{3}	kilo	k
10^{2}	hecto	h
10^{1}	deca	da
10^{-1}	deci	d
10^{-2}	centi	c
10^{-3}	milli	m
10^{-6}	micro	μ
10^{-9}	nano	n
10^{-12}	pico	p
10^{-15}	femto	f
10^{-18}	atto	a
10^{-21}	zepto	z
10^{-24}	yocto	y

11.3 Basic and derived units

Table of basic units

Physical quantity	Dimensions	S. I. unit	Symbol
mass	M	kilogram	kg
length	L	metre	m
time	T	second	s
amount of substance	dimensionless	mole	mol
electric current	I	ampère	A
temperature	θ	kelvin	K
luminous intensity	C	candela	cd

Table of supplimentary units

Physical quantity	Dimensions	S. I. unit	Symbol
angle	dimensionless	radian	rad
		degree	°
solid angle	dimensionless	steradian	sr

$$2\pi \, \text{rad} = 360°; \quad 1 \, \text{rad} = 57.296°$$

Table of derived units

Physical quantity	Dimensions	S. I. unit (symbol)
area	L^2	m^2
volume	L^3	m^3
frequency	T^{-1}	hertz(Hz)
speed	LT^{-1}	ms^{-1}
acceleration	LT^{-2}	ms^{-2}
angular speed	T^{-1}	rads^{-1}
angular acceleration	T^{-2}	rads^{-2}
density	ML^{-3}	kgm^{-3}
momentum	MLT^{-1}	kgms^{-1}
moment of inertia	ML^2	kgm^2
angular momentum	ML^2T^{-1}	kgm^{2}s^{-1}
force	MLT^{-2}	newton(N)
torque, moment of force	ML^2T^{-2}	Nm
energy, work	ML^2T^{-2}	joule(J)Nm
pressure, stress	$ML^{-1}T^{-2}$	pascal(Pa)Nm^{-2}
power, radiant flux	ML^2T^{-3}	watt(W)Js^{-1}
viscosity (dynamic)	$ML^{-1}T^{-1}$	Pas
surface tension	MT^{-2}	Nm^{-1}
electric charge	TI	coulomb(C)
electric potential	$ML^2T^{-3}I^{-1}$	volt(V)WA^{-1}
electric resistance	$ML^2T^{-3}I^{-2}$	ohm(Ω)VA^{-1}
electric conductance	$M^{-1}L^{-2}T^3I^2$	siemens(S)
electric field strengh	$MLT^{-3}I^{-1}$	Vm^{-1}
electric charge density	$L^{-3}TI$	Cm^{-3}
electric flux density	$L^{-2}TI$	Cm^{-2}
capacitance	$M^{-1}L^{-2}T^4I^2$	farad(F)AsV^{-1}
magnetic flux	$ML^2T^{-2}I^{-1}$	weber(Wb)
magnetic flux density	$MT^{-2}I^{-1}$	tesla(T)Wbm^{-2}
inductance	$ML^2T^{-2}I^{-2}$	henry(H)WbA^{-1}
permittivity(ϵ)	$M^{-1}L^{-3}T^4I^2$	Fm^{-1}
permeability(μ)	$MLT^{-2}I^{-2}$	Hm^{-1}
quantity of heat	ML^2T^{-2}	joule(J)
heat capacity, entropy	$ML^2T^{-2}\theta^{-1}$	JK^{-1}
specific heat capacity, specific entropy	$L^2T^{-2}\theta^{-1}$	Jkg^{-1}K^{-1}
radiant flux density	MT^{-3}	Wm^{-2}
thermal conductivity	$MLT^{-3}\theta^{-1}$	Wm^{-1}K^{-1}
latent heat	L^2T^{-2}	Jkg^{-1}
molar energy	ML^2T^{-2}	Jmol^{-1}
molar entropy, molar heat capacity	$ML^2T^{-2}\theta^{-1}$	Jmol^{-1}K^{-1}
luminous flux(1cd=1l$_{\mathrm{m}}$ sr^{-1})	ML^2T^{-3}	lumen(l$_{\mathrm{m}}$)
illuminance	MT^{-2}	lux(l$_{\mathrm{x}}$)

11.4 Values of some physical constants

Quantity	Symbol	Value
speed of light in a vacuum	$c = (\epsilon_0\mu_0)^{-\frac{1}{2}}$	$2.99792458 \times 10^8 \mathrm{ms}^{-1}$
permeability of a vacuum	μ_0	$4\pi \times 10^{-7} \mathrm{Hm}^{-1}$
permittivity of a vacuum	ϵ_0	$8.854187817 \times 10^{-12} \mathrm{FM}^{-1}$
elementary charge	e	$1.60217733 \times 10^{-19} \mathrm{C}$
Coulomb force constant	k_e	$8.9875 \times 10^9 \mathrm{Nm}^2\mathrm{C}^{-2}$
fine structure constant	$\alpha = e^2/(4\pi\epsilon_0\hbar c)$	$1/137.0$
gravitational constant	G	$6.67258 \times 10^{-11} \mathrm{m}^3\mathrm{kg}^{-1}\mathrm{s}^{-2}$
atomic mass unit	u	$1.6605402 \times 10^{-27} \mathrm{kg}$
energy equivalent of u		$931.494 \mathrm{MeV}$
rest mass of electron	m_e	$9.1093897 \times 10^{-31} \mathrm{kg}$
		$0.0005486 \mathrm{u}$
electron rest energy	$m_e c^2$	$0.5109991 \mathrm{MeV}$
rest mass of proton	m_p	$1.6726231 \times 10^{-27} \mathrm{kg}$
		$1.007276 \mathrm{u}$
proton rest energy	$m_p c^2$	$938.27231 \mathrm{MeV}$
rest mass of neutron	m_n	$1.6749286 \times 10^{-27} \mathrm{kg}$
		$1.008665 \mathrm{u}$
neutron rest energy	$m_n c^2$	$939.56563 \mathrm{MeV}$
Planck's constant	h	$6.626075 \times 10^{-34} \mathrm{Js}$
	$\hbar = h/(2\pi)$	$1.05457266 \times 10^{-34} \mathrm{Js}$
Rydberg energy	$R_\infty = \alpha^2 m_e c^2/2$	$13.61 \mathrm{eV}$
Bohr radius	a_0	$5.29177249 \times 10^{-11} \mathrm{m}$
Compton wavelength of electron	λ_C	$2.42631058 \times 10^{-12} \mathrm{m}$
Avogadro constant	N_A	$6.0221367 \times 10^{23} \mathrm{mol}^{-1}$
Boltzmann constant	k	$1.380658 \times 10^{-23} \mathrm{JK}^{-1}$
Stefan-Boltzmann constant	σ	$5.67052 \times 10^{-8} \mathrm{Wm}^{-2}\mathrm{K}^{-4}$
Wien's (displacement law) constant		$2.8978 \times 10^{-3} \mathrm{mK}$
Bohr constant	μ_B	$9.2740154 \times 10^{-24} \mathrm{JT}^{-1}$
nuclear magneton	μ_N	$5.05057866 \times 10^{-27} \mathrm{JT}^{-1}$
triple point temperature	T_t	$273.16 \mathrm{K}$
molar gas constant	R	$8.315 \mathrm{JK}^{-1}\mathrm{mol}^{-1}$
micron	$\mu\mathrm{m}$	$10^{-6} \mathrm{m}$
ångström	Å	$10^{-10} \mathrm{m}$
femtometre or fermi	fm	$10^{-15} \mathrm{m}$
barn	b	$10^{-28} \mathrm{m}^2$

11.5 Useful masses

The atomic mass unit, u, is defined to be $\frac{1}{12}$ of the mass of the Carbon-12 atom.

Table of particle masses

particle/atom		mass
p	m_{p}	$= 1.6726231 \times 10^{-27}\mathrm{kg}$
		$= 1.007276\mathrm{u}$
		$= 938.272\mathrm{MeV/c}^2$
e	m_{e}	$= 9.1093897 \times 10^{-31}\mathrm{kg}$
		$= 0.0005486\mathrm{u}$
		$= 0.511\mathrm{MeV/c}^2$
n	m_{n}	$= 1.6749286 \times 10^{-27}\mathrm{kg}$
		$= 1.008665\mathrm{u}$
		$= 939.566\mathrm{MeV/c}^2$
$^{1}_{1}\mathrm{H}$		$1.007825\mathrm{u}$
$^{2}_{1}\mathrm{H}$		$2.014102\mathrm{u}$
$^{3}_{1}\mathrm{H}$		$3.016049\mathrm{u}$
$^{3}_{2}\mathrm{He}$		$3.016029\mathrm{u}$
$^{4}_{2}\mathrm{He}$		$4.002603\mathrm{u}$
$^{6}_{3}\mathrm{Li}$		$6.015121\mathrm{u}$
$^{7}_{3}\mathrm{Li}$		$7.016003\mathrm{u}$
$^{12}_{5}\mathrm{B}$		$12.014352\mathrm{u}$
$^{12}_{6}\mathrm{C}$		$12.000000\mathrm{u}$
$^{13}_{6}\mathrm{C}$		$13.003355\mathrm{u}$
$^{14}_{6}\mathrm{C}$		$14.003242\mathrm{u}$
$^{12}_{7}\mathrm{N}$		$12.018613\mathrm{u}$
$^{13}_{7}\mathrm{N}$		$13.005738\mathrm{u}$
$^{14}_{7}\mathrm{N}$		$14.003074\mathrm{u}$
$^{92}_{36}\mathrm{Kr}$		$91.8973\mathrm{u}$
$^{141}_{56}\mathrm{Ba}$		$140.9139\mathrm{u}$
$^{210}_{84}\mathrm{Po}$		$209.982848\mathrm{u}$
$^{218}_{84}\mathrm{Po}$		$218.008965\mathrm{u}$
$^{220}_{86}\mathrm{Rn}$		$220.011369\mathrm{u}$
$^{222}_{86}\mathrm{Rn}$		$222.017574\mathrm{u}$
$^{224}_{88}\mathrm{Ra}$		$224.020187\mathrm{u}$
$^{226}_{88}\mathrm{Ra}$		$226.025402\mathrm{u}$
$^{227}_{90}\mathrm{Th}$		$227.027701\mathrm{u}$
$^{228}_{90}\mathrm{Th}$		$228.028716\mathrm{u}$
$^{230}_{90}\mathrm{Th}$		$230.033127\mathrm{u}$
$^{231}_{91}\mathrm{Pa}$		$231.035880\mathrm{u}$
$^{234}_{90}\mathrm{Th}$		$234.043593\mathrm{u}$
$^{235}_{92}\mathrm{U}$		$235.043924\mathrm{u}$
$^{238}_{92}\mathrm{U}$		$238.050784\mathrm{u}$
$^{235}_{93}\mathrm{Np}$		$235.044057\mathrm{u}$

11.6 Astronomical constants

Mass of Earth	m_E	5.976×10^{24}kg
Radius of Earth (equatorial)	R_E	6.378×10^6m
Gravity at Earth's surface	g	9.80665ms^{-2}
Mass of Sun	$M_\odot$	1.989×10^{30}kg
Radius of Sun	$R_\odot$	6.9599×10^8m
Solar effective temperature	T_e	5800K
Luminosity of Sun	$L_\odot$	3.826×10^{26}W
Astronomical unit	AU	1.496×10^{11}m
Parsec	pc	3.086×10^{16}m
Jansky	Jy	10^{-26}Wm^{-2}Hz^{-1}
Tropical year		3.1557×10^7s
Standard atmosphere	atm	101325Pa

11.7 Mathematical constants

pi (Archimedes' constant)	π	3.141 592 653 793
exponential constant	e	2.718 281 828 459
Apery's constant	$\zeta(3)$	1.202 056 903 160
Catalan's constant	K	0.915 965 594 177
Dottie's number	r	0.739 085 133 215
Euler's constant	γ	0.577 215 664 902
Feigenbaum's constant	α	2.502 907 875 096
Feigenbaum's constant	δ	4.669 201 609 102
Gelfond's constant	e^π	23.140 692 632 78
Gibb's constant	G	1.851 937 051 982
Golden mean	ϕ	1.618 033 988 750
Khintchine's constant	K	2.685 452 001 065
omega constant	Ω	0.567 143 290 410
parabolic constant	P_2	2.295 587 149 393
plastic constant	P	1.324 717 957 245
Sierpiński's constant	K	2.584 981 759 579
Trott's constant	T_2	0.108 410 151 223
Wallis's constant	W	2.094 551 481 542

11.8 The Greek alphabet

Letter	lowercase	uppercase
Alpha	α	A
Beta	β	B
Gamma	γ	Γ
Delta	δ	Δ
Epsilon	ϵ	E
Zeta	ζ	Z
Eta	η	H
Theta	θ	Θ
Iota	ι	I
Kappa	κ	K
Lambda	λ	Λ
Mu	μ	M
Nu	ν	N
Xi	ξ	Ξ
Omicron	o	O
Pi	π	Π
Rho	ρ	P
Sigma	σ	Σ
Tau	τ	T
Upsilon	υ	Y
Phi	ϕ, φ	Φ
Chi	χ	X
Psi	ψ	Ψ
Omega	ω, ϖ	Ω

Index